T0066854

Funky Lily's

MIND CANDY
&
SOUL FOOD

Praise for *Funky Lily's Shorts*

"Congratulations—I was overwhelmed! Great fun to read, to the life moments behind the book and to your remarkable life philosophy that was leading your pen. A good book makes you immortal—the rest of us will just fade away."

—R. Horvath, PhD

"I must tell you how very much I enjoyed your book! I admire your sense of adventure, your determination, your ability to rise above adverse situations. Going from Molly in "Death of a Dog" to "Funky Lily the Clown" is beyond belief. Thanks so much for sharing your life."   —M. Weinstein, Writer

"Your "Slices of Life" got me in such depth of feeling: I thought how pain in one's life can turn us to hate and tempt us to inflict the same pain on others. Or, it can turn us to be sensitive and compassionate. I believe that some of those painful experiences have made you into the self-confident and caring woman that you are..."   —M. Carcamo, OISE Teacher

"I so very much enjoyed your "Shorts"... Your delight in the human comedy shines everywhere but also your profound empathy with the sorrowful souls that surround us. Your book wrought a positive change in me and probably does in everyone who reads it, and that should satisfy you."   —M. VanEvery, Poet

"I was really moved with the content of what you say, but also with the form of your narrative which makes it all so graphic. Your narratives about Cuba and Mexico are very sensitive, and some of your stories about Mexico are hilarious—good that you can take it all with humour! Lilian, I did enjoy your book a lot—I laughed and I cried."   —Margarita C.

"Lilian, I really enjoyed your many good stories, witty stories, and touching stories, it's a pleasure to read them. I thought the characters were wonderful, so I really got involved in the stories. Thanks for sharing it all with the world!"

—K. McConnaughey, Editor

"Planning to do something new every year is such a good idea, and I like the philosophy of the 6th day of an 8-day holiday, getting out the list of things to do. It's giving us all something to think about. Well done!"

—J. Doyne, Toastmaster

Funky Lily's
MIND CANDY
&
SOUL FOOD

**A thought-provoking collection of
short stories, essays, and free verse**

Lilian Marton

Order this book online at www.trafford.com
or email orders@trafford.com

Most Trafford titles are also available at major online book retailers.

© Copyright 2014 Lilian Marton.

Design & Layout: Beth Crane, WeMakeBooks.ca
Author Photo: Julianna

All rights reserved. No part of this publication may be reproduced,
stored in a retrieval system, or transmitted, in any form or by
any means, electronic, mechanical, photocopying, recording, or
otherwise, without the written prior permission of the author.

Printed in the United States of America.

ISBN: 978-1-4907-3024-0 (sc)
ISBN: 978-1-4907-3025-7 (e)

Library of Congress Control Number: 2014904983

Because of the dynamic nature of the Internet, any web addresses or
links contained in this book may have changed since publication and
may no longer be valid. The views expressed in this work are solely those
of the author and do not necessarily reflect the views of the publisher,
and the publisher hereby disclaims any responsibility for them.

Any people depicted in stock imagery provided by Thinkstock are models,
and such images are being used for illustrative purposes only.
Certain stock imagery © Thinkstock.

Trafford rev. 03/13/2014

Trafford PUBLISHING® www.trafford.com
North America & international
toll-free: 1 888 232 4444 (USA & Canada)
fax: 812 355 4082

To George

my husband of many years and best friend

for never clipping my wings

and letting me fly

Contents

Preface

In the overall scheme of things, not much has changed since my last book, *Funky Lily's Shorts*. Life is still short, and it's still getting shorter faster than ever, and I'm still getting older. That's wonderful, considering the alternative.

The major change is that a broken hip brought my clowning 'career' to a screeching halt, especially as I had been a self-designated dancing clown for a dozen years or so. And it certainly curtailed our ballroom dancing, affecting my husband much more than me, as I had been dancing all my life.

Perhaps that's why this book, *Funky Lily's Mind Candy & Soul Food*, ended up with a rather different focus. Its tone is much more reflective, more spiritual, more appreciative of life's positive aspects. Oh, the humour is still pushing through—you can't keep a clown down for long!

BLESSINGS emphasizes a more spiritual approach to daily life, pointing out that blessings can be found—and enjoyed—in almost everything. It's all a matter of cultivating the right attitude.

VERSE-ABILITY is a fascinating first-time experiment in Free Verse, with different styles and meters, creative reflections and reminiscences, and with generous dashes of imagination. It may leave the reader wondering: Is it intensely personal? Or just wild fantasy?

INSPIRED PERSPECTIVES is a combination of autobiographical stories, creative non-fiction, and more thought-provoking essays. More food for thought.

My anagram, Mollina Tarin, is also making an appearance again, as she did in the last book. She will, of course, stay with me for the rest of our lives together. However, Funky Lily the Clown is taking a back seat for now.

It is totally up to you, discerning reader, to decide which parts of this book are Mind Candy and which are Soul Food.

Lilian Marton
a.k.a. Funky Lily the Clown
a.k.a. Mollina Tarin: "Molly"

Author permission at: funkylily@aol.com

Blessings

Adversity—An Old Story

A man found the cocoon of a butterfly in his garden and, intrigued, he followed its progress on a daily basis.

Then, one day, a small opening appeared in the cocoon. As he watched the butterfly over several hours as it struggled to force its body through that tiny hole, it seemed to him that it wasn't making any progress at all any more, that it had gotten as far as it possibly could, and that it could go no further.

So the man decided to help the butterfly. He got some scissors and snipped off the remaining bit of the cocoon, and he was rewarded with seeing the butterfly emerge easily.

However, he noticed that the butterfly had a grotesquely swollen body and tiny, shriveled wings. But he expected that, in no time, the wings would grow and expand in order to support the body that would then contract to a normal size. But as he checked every day, he realized that nothing was changing at all. The body remained swollen and the wings tiny and useless. He was at a loss to understand what was happening.

The butterfly spent the rest of its life crawling around the ground with its swollen body and shriveled, useless wings. It was never able to fly!

What the man with his good intentions did not understand was that the struggle necessary for the butterfly to get through the tiny opening of the cocoon was nature's way of forcing fluid from the body of the butterfly into its wings, so that it would be ready for flight once it was free of the cocoon.

✢

Although many of us are already familiar with this story, we may have forgotten the valuable lesson it teaches us, that struggle is exactly what we need in our lives.

If we were allowed to go through life without any obstacles, it would cripple us. We would not be as strong as we could have been. We would be crawling around at mediocre levels, never developing and giving flight to our wings, to our dreams. We could never fly!

As an unknown author once wrote:

- I asked for Strength… and I was given difficulties to overcome.
- I asked for Wisdom… and I was given problems to solve.
- I asked for Prosperity… and I was given brains and brawn to work.
- I asked for Courage… and I was given danger to overcome.
- I asked for Love… and I was given troubled people to help.
- I asked for Favors… and I was given opportunities.
- I received nothing I wanted… but I received everything I needed.

✝

As we reflect back on our life, how did WE emerge from our cocoon? Did someone take scissors to our cocoon to snip it open and make life easy and pleasant for us, removing all obstacles for us, and perhaps leaving us soft and dependent in the process? Did we grow up pampered and spoiled, never wanting anything before it was given to us? Were we the envy of our peers, always owning the latest in trends? Did we end up emotionally and spiritually fragile and stunted, in a self-limiting state of victim mentality, without realizing it?

Or do we thank our lucky stars that we had to struggle through at least part of our life on our own? That we had to work to put ourselves through school, to pay for our own possessions and travels, and to become responsible for ourselves and our own destiny?

Do we realize that this struggle to emerge from our cocoon on our own—a struggle we possibly resented at the time—was what we needed to make us strong and wise and resilient and compassionate and ready to cope with the challenges of life? Are we grateful that such adversity has allowed us to build character fortitude and soul stamina?

Then we realize that often what we want is not what we need—but it is exactly what we need to learn in order to mature and grow and become useful and contributing members of society.

✝

"There is no education like adversity."
—Benjamin Disraeli, British Statesman

✝ ✝ ✝

Blissful Blackout

During 2004s brightest full moon, the Harvest Moon near the end of September, we had an unusual and long blackout in our area of the city. For about two and a half hours, entire neighborhoods waited in the dark for the lights to come back on—which they finally did at 10 PM—and, no doubt, this blackout inconvenienced, or at least annoyed, a good many people.

We had planned to watch a taped movie later in the family room downstairs as my husband had decided not to participate in his usual Tuesday night Chess Club game. And then, suddenly, everything stopped. The dishwasher died with a desperate gurgle in the middle of a cycle. The CNN reporter was rudely silenced in mid-sentence about a Botox tragedy in Hollywood—we may never know what happened to that poor rich woman who didn't get the results she had expected. I went groping for our powerful lantern on a shelf downstairs, then went around the house turning off the lights and anything else that might have been turned on, in order not to overload the system unnecessarily once the power came back on.

Suddenly I remembered: it was full moon, still! I had already fallen under its spell the night before as I was driving home from my monthly Clown Alley meeting. So I installed myself in front of the living room picture window, pulled back the curtains, and watched the majestic full moon just beginning to rise above the dark bushes across the road. Comfortably settled in a chair, with my feet up on the windowsill, I sat gazing at the moon, marveling at the unusual, all-encompassing silence that allowed me to meditate and contemplate life.

Then, softly and romantically, my husband started playing the piano in the dark, enhancing the magical mood. Thank God for pianos! Electric keyboards would be useless tonight, but acoustic pianos can be played in the dark, the same way blind people play. We both remembered blind George Shearing who became a world-renowned pianist after losing his sight at age six, and who is still performing in his eighties now.

After a while, the dark was not so dark any more, so I left the powerful lantern on standby. What a wonderfully soothing but eerie silence in the neighborhood! No appliances running, no air-conditioners humming, virtually no traffic, nothing—just pure, sacred silence. The mysterious man in the moon seemed to be smiling; perhaps he was finally getting the attention he deserved. Then I remembered that, during the last massive blackout, we also had a full moon. Could there be a connection?

Slowly I began to distinguish details in the dark. There was just enough moonlight to allow me to jot down my thoughts on paper, without really seeing what I was writing. After a while I saw the gaslight on the lawn across the street like a faint star in a dark universe. Then some leaves dancing on a bush looked like two playful dolphins jumping across the face of the moon. Without streetlights, the headlights of an occasional car were carefully groping their way around the winding neighborhood streets. Sharp clouds in the sky were strangely illuminated by the slowly rising moon. Some neighbors were venturing out onto their porches to enjoy the brilliant, silent beauty of it all.

All too soon for me, the moon had risen high enough in the sky to disappear over our roof and thus deprive me of my writing light. And while many people were upset about having to change their plans for the evening, my two hours of meditating and enjoying soft piano music and writing by moonlight had provided me with the most blissful of blackouts.

✚ ✚ ✚

Life's Little Miracles

Yes, I believe in miracles.

Oh, I'm not talking about the miraculous power of a lowly weed breaking open solid asphalt to push its eager young blades into daylight for survival and growth.

Nor about the incredible colors of a winter sunset, with a giant orange ball of fire slipping gently through layers of pink and mauve and deep purple into temporary oblivion.

Not even about the most impossible parking space becoming available the very moment you need it, simply because you asked for it ('Thank you, Universe, for a parking spot near that entrance…').

No, I'm talking about wish-fulfilling miracles—the kind when you want something so badly that it actually comes to happen.

Like the time I took an excursion by bus from Cancun to Chichen Itza, the famous ancient Mayan temple site on Mexico's Yucatan peninsula.

I was the only one from our metaphysics study group to take this excursion. The others were either visiting Tulum, another archeological site south of Cancun, or simply taking advantage of our day off to swim and sunbathe.

The tour bus was almost full; I was one of the few singles occupying a double seat. I really wanted to sit in the very front seat, next to our tour guide José, but that seat was reserved for the guide's briefcase full of notes and books and probably lunch.

I had been briefed about José. He was Mayan Indian, about 35, short and a bit stocky, apparently an authority on Maya philosophy and culture, and very spiritual. Oh, how I wanted to sit next to him and learn from him first-hand! But nobody was ever allowed in that seat—a sort of unwritten rule.

On the outskirts of Cancun we stopped to pick up two more passengers who had missed the previous bus. As there were no more double seats available for the couple, José evaluated the singles in the double seats, then headed straight toward me.

"I'm very sorry to bother you," he said politely. "But would you mind giving your seat to this couple and sit next to me in the front? I do hope this is not too inconvenient for you."

"No problem at all," I replied, my heart leaping in my chest. "I would love to sit with you!"

For the next two hours until we reached Chichen Itza, and for the entire trip back after exploring the temple site, José and I discussed philosophy and metaphysics and compared our respective ways of life.

José was very proud of his Maya heritage, even though the Mayas of today lead a very poor and largely primitive and oppressed existence—a mere shadow of their former highly developed civilization. But it was the Mayas who invented a system of hieroglyphics, an accurate calendar, and something we have been taking for granted ever since: the number zero. (We can only imagine how complex calculations would be without a zero!) And, as Chichen Itza and numerous other archeological sites demonstrate, the Mayas, basically an agricultural people, were also master architects and artists.

José showed me the true beauty of the basic Maya philosophy: Living in close communion with nature, forever respectful of nature, never taking more of nature's abundance than what is needed for personal use, never abusing or raping nature.

What a simple yet very difficult concept! Simple when you are poor, but difficult when you are living in a materialistic world where the lure of greed is everywhere, where you take more than you need in order to make an extra buck and get ahead of the other guy. Perhaps this is the price we pay for progress; perhaps it was an inevitable evolution.

Once again I got a deeper insight into the Mexican soul, as I do on every one of my Mexican trips—but this time thanks to a miracle. There were several singles occupying a double seat on our bus, and José could have asked any of us to sit with him. Or he could have asked two of us to double up. But instead, his very intuitive Maya Indian spirit sensed my deep wish—and fulfilled it.

✝ ✝ ✝

"Coincidence is when your God works a miracle
and chooses to remain anonymous."

— Anon

To The Past Men In My Life

Thank you all for having taught me the following lessons over the years, even if we were not aware of it at the time—lessons I continue to learn.

1. "Follow Your Heart" can be very bad advice, because it can lead to a broken heart and mangled emotions and sorrow.

2. I should never cry over somebody who would not cry over me—and you certainly never shed a tear over me.

3. No matter how deeply I love somebody, that somebody may never love me back. So I accept that fact and move on.

4. However much I may have grieved over losing you at the time, I also realized that I could not lose what I never had.

5. In matters of the heart, there are givers and there are takers, and I'm a giver—which is never any guarantee for reciprocation.

6. Love always involves risk, and I prefer to love and take the risk of getting hurt. Getting cold and jaded instead would be no life at all for me. I like Teflon coating only on my cookware, not on my heart. That's a choice we have to make in life: Get hurt, or get Teflon-coated.

7. Although you occupied too much space in my head and heart for a time, I must remain honest and outspoken, because I cannot be who I am not. I have to stay true to myself, even if you were unable to accept that. That's another choice I made.

8. When you told me that we must accept a loved one uncon-ditionally, but as you obviously never accepted me as I was, it just proved that you never truly cared.

9. No matter how much two people seem to have in common, if one is unwilling to see and move beyond some inevitable differences, these two can remain worlds apart.

10. If breaking up leaves me with the phantom limb syndrome—still feeling the pain in the amputated limb—I simply remember to put things in perspective: I have survived far greater calamities than a lost relationship.

As a result of learning these lessons, I discovered that part of my purpose in life is to be a catalyst. I remember one of you asking me in exasperation: "Must you always be my conscience?!"

This way, over the years I have helped change the lives of some friends and relatives in a positive way: A catalyst can create change without basically changing its own nature.

Therefore, thanks to all of you. Although I have been happily married for many years, you will always remain part of my Being.

✛ ✛ ✛

Ponderables

As beauty is in the eye of the beholder, so also are hard times in the mind of the beholder.

True wisdom lies in discerning the meaning within all things in life.

Nothing can come to us that we do not have the strength to meet and handle successfully.

Good or bad—every experience in our lives is a gift to ourselves.

Let us trust the process of life. We are safe: it is OK to let go. Let us trust the wisdom of the Universe.

Let us learn to write our hurts in the sand where the winds of forgiveness can blow them away. But let us carve our blessings in stone where no wind can ever erase it.

Expand and open your mind to accept change, because change is the only constant in the Universe.

If we like who we are today, then let us release the past with love, because we are the result of our past.

The secret to knowing our future is to create it for ourselves today.

Remember that people respond to their perception of reality, not to reality itself.

☩ ☩ ☩

Reflections

Look at everything as if you were seeing and experiencing it for the first time, and live each day as if it were your last, and your life will be filled with wonderment and joy.

Your thoughts become words; words become actions; actions become habits; habits become your character; your character becomes your destiny. Therefore, watch your thoughts.

You reveal your true character by the choices you make and the promises you keep. What you say and do will define who you are.

Consciously celebrate and be grateful for each day. Recognize and reflect upon your blessings. Don't dwell on the past: don't allow yourself to be a victim of your past. Move on.

Tough times never last. Tough people do.

No matter how much or how little you have, contentment in life comes with appreciating what you already have. Many people have plenty but can never be content because they always want more.

Take responsibility for what and who you are.

When you bring love, light and joy into the lives of others, it will come back into your own. Let your light shine.

✟ ✟ ✟

Seven Favorite Affirmations

to contemplate daily

✝

Today is a wonderful day because I choose to make it so.

I will consciously celebrate and be grateful for each day.

To a greater or lesser extent, we influence every person we meet. Therefore, I always try to be a positive and loving influence.

I will always strive to be part of the solution, not part of the problem.

Nobody can take advantage of me, or diminish my self-esteem in any way, without my consent.

I release the past with love because I like the way I am today—and I am the result of my past.

The most important thing in life is to discern what is important, and what is not.

✝

Silent Messenger

Looking around in the picture gallery while waiting for my newly framed pictures to be wrapped, my eyes were suddenly held captive by a winter scene high up on the wall.

There was a snow-covered forest of birch trees, with a white tiger moving silently and stealthily in the snow among the birches. It was a study in different shades of white, the only dark spots being the notches on the white birch bark and the stripes on the white tiger. Then there were his intense, incredibly blue eyes! I stood mesmerized, and suddenly tears welled up in my eyes.

What was happening to me? I tried to look away, but couldn't… And my tears kept flowing.

The Korean store owner looked at me, concerned. "You OK?" he asked.

"I must have this painting," I finally said, having just come to that conclusion and trying to figure out how to pay for it just before Christmas and a winter vacation. "Can you give me a good price?" He started calculating and came up with a figure. "I'm afraid that's still a bit too much for me right now," I ventured. But I didn't dare leave the painting there for another time. What if someone else bought it in the meantime? Every time I looked at it, my tears started flowing again, so it definitely held a message for me. "Can you at least leave off the taxes?" The Korean started calculating again. Finally he came up with a price I was willing and able to handle.

Then, suddenly, it hit me: where was I going to hang it? Mentally I started scanning all the appropriate walls in our house.

I needed a space where I could look at it anytime, as often as I wanted or needed to, not in a hallway or in a seldom used room. And I didn't want to move any current pictures which were all where they needed to be. In the end, there remained only one empty wall: in the freshly painted kitchen where we had not yet put back any previous decorations.

YES! As the kitchen table is often my favorite place to work because the south-west view through the walk-out doors to the deck and onto the evergreen back yard is so lovely and inspiring, this wall turned out to be the ideal place for my study in white.

Now, any time I enter the kitchen, my beautiful, mysterious white tiger is waiting for me. I realized I needed to title the painting, so after lengthy contemplation I decided to call it "Silent Messenger" even if only as a temporary working title.

I don't yet know what the tiger's ultimate silent message is, but I know there is one. So far, different messages have come to me in layers. As I have discovered, I must have my eyes WIDE open to see the white tiger in the snowy white birch forest, or I hardly see him. Squint, and he is just an illusion—gone—the exact opposite of my husband's painting of the Mona Lisa in mosaic style where you have to squint in order to see her. In other words, I need to keep my spiritual eyes open to see through the illusion.

So, whatever the message, it is certainly not obvious, but it is there, and my senses need to be wide open and receptive. That is probably the initial message. Also, I feel that the subsequent, deeper messages will be different for every viewer who is willing to look further.

Researching its symbolism, I discovered that the white tiger is solitary and nocturnal, that its cycle of power is during the full moon and the new moon, that it is a mystical animal usually seen only as a glimpse in the snow. It symbolizes royalty and strength, passion and power, devotion and sensuality, and a spirituality and mysticism that suggest a spiritual life lifting its soul above the material world. The Buddhists consider it a symbol of spiritual illumination, and its solitary nature is seen as a symbol of chastity.

This magnificent animal with its sleek and powerful muscles and soft, thick coat is said to stimulate thoughts of sensuality, and awaken a new sensuality, a sensitivity to touch. The appearance of a white tiger in your life is said to awaken new passion, and that power, renewed devotion and adventures will manifest in your life.

As I keep peeling back further layers of meaning, I discover a number of similarities with my own nature. Like most writers and other artists, I also have a solitary streak, and all my life I have felt particularly sensitive and receptive during the full moon. My spiritual life is definitely more important to me than materialism, and increasingly so, and my passion and devotion have been redirected into more uplifting and rewarding projects over the years, leading to new adventures.

Thank you, silent messenger!

✝ ✝ ✝

The Blessing Of Problems

We all encounter problems in life, and most of us hate them. After all, they upset our often complacent rhythm of daily life.

But—have you ever thought about the positive side of problems?

Just think: Problems give us the opportunity to become acquainted with and test our capabilities. They give us a chance to learn yet another lesson to help us develop and grow as human beings.

When everything goes smoothly, we rarely think about what we are really capable of, and how far we can stretch our talents and resources. It is only when we run into hurdles or problems that we mobilize our energies, and we are often surprised at our strengths and capabilities.

It is in solving difficult problems that we usually derive our greatest satisfaction.

So, next time you encounter a problem, look at the other side of the problem and ask: What can I learn from this? What lesson is this teaching me? How can this help me grow and stretch?

Therefore, let us be grateful for the problems in our life. Let's look at them this way:

A problem is a blessing disguised as a lesson.

✦

"We can't solve problems by using the same kind of thinking we used when we created them."

—Albert Einstein, Mathematical Physicist

✦ ✦ ✦

What's Important In Life

(by Author unknown—with thanks!)

Sometimes people come into your life and you know right away that they were meant to be there, to serve some sort of purpose, to teach you a lesson, or to help you figure out who you are or who you want to become.

You never know who these people may be—a roommate, a neighbor, a professor, a friend, a lover, or even a complete stranger—but when you lock eyes with them, you know at that very moment they will affect your life in some profound way.

Sometimes things happen to you that may seem horrible, painful, and unfair at first, but in reflection you find that without overcoming those obstacles you would have never realized your potential, strength, willpower, or heart.

Illness, injury, love, lost moments of true greatness, and sheer stupidity all occur to test the limits of your soul. Without these small tests, whatever they may be, life would be like a smoothly paved, straight, flat road to nowhere. It would be safe and comfortable, but dull and utterly pointless.

The people you meet who affect your life, and the success and downfalls you experience, help create who you are and who you become. Even the bad experiences can be learned from. In fact, they are often the most important ones.

If someone loves you, give love back to them in whatever way you can, not only because they love you, but because, in a way, they are teaching you to love and how to open your heart and eyes to things.

If someone hurts you, betrays you, or breaks your heart, forgive them, for they have helped you learn about trust and the importance of being cautious to whom you open your heart.

Make every day count. Appreciate every moment and take from those moments everything that you possibly can, for you many never be able to experience it again. Talk to people that you have never talked to before, and listen to what they have to say.

Let yourself fall in love, break free, and set your sights high. Hold your head up because you have every right to. Tell yourself you are a great individual and believe in yourself, for if you don't believe in yourself, it will be hard for others to believe in you.

You can make anything you wish of your life. Create your own life and then go out and live it with absolutely no regrets.

And if you love someone, tell them, for you never know what tomorrow may have in store.

✢

Learn a lesson in life each day that you live.

Today is the tomorrow you were worried about yesterday.
Think about it: Was it worth it?

✢ ✢ ✢

Verse-Ability

Free Verse

Free verse is full of contradictions.

It is a 'modern' form of un-metered poetry that has existed for centuries. Ancient Hebrew poets are said to have used it in their Psalms, and the French Symbolist poets of the late 1800s coined the term 'vers libre' to describe their verse technique. In modern times it has regained popularity because it leaves the poet so much more creative freedom.

It has no set rules. Each poet is free to make up different rules for each poem, not being bound by traditional forms. However, it should still contain the elements of beautiful prose.

Although strongly rhythmic, it doesn't rhyme, and it lacks a formal metric pattern, but well-written free verse will create its own rhythm and sound patterns. Unlike conventional forms of poetry, the rhythm and pattern in free verse are created entirely by the poet, but often following natural speech patterns.

There is still the basic rule that, like other forms of poetry, free verse should present its message in colorful mental images and carefully chosen words. Emphasis can be created with pattern and sound repetition to achieve a lyrical quality.

The following is an experimentation of such un-metered verse. Enjoy!

✝ ✝ ✝

A Clown's Prayer

As I stumble through this life
Help me create more laughter than tears
Dispense more happiness than gloom
Spread more cheer than despair

Never let me become so indifferent
That I will fail to see
The wonder in the eyes of a child
Or gratitude in the eyes of the aged

Never let me forget that my total effort
Is to cheer people, make them happy
And let them forget at least momentarily
All the unpleasantness in their lives

And in my final moment
May I hear You whisper:
"When you made My people smile
You made Me smile"

(Author Unknown)

☩ ☩ ☩

Moonstruck

The moon, just past its halfway waxing cycle,
Comically appearing slightly bulging,
A gently pregnant half moon in anticipation
Of its brilliant fullness within days

Now hanging carefree in the dusky sky
Still punctuated with lingering clouds,
Wispy, quickly vanishing pink clouds,
Memories of an earlier lovely sunset.

An unspoken pact made eons ago
With a fantasy lover in a faraway land
That both would gaze upon the full moon
Thinking of the other, remembering

When for a flicker in eternity
We intersected in that vast
Mysterious grid of the Universe
Never to be the same again, ever.

So each full moon would trigger
Long buried memories, secret longings,
Unfulfilled dreams, fantasies and
Sadly unrealistic hopes.

Oh glorious, intoxicating full moon,
Forever my trusty accomplice and
Silent witness to my innermost stirrings:
Shine on brilliantly into eternity!

☩ ☩ ☩

My Source Of Being

A grand moment of ecstasy
Snatched from everyday concerns
Fully living in the NOW, now
Connecting to the ever-present Source
So often forgotten and overlooked
In the bustle and business
Of an ego-dominated world

Thousands of people all around
Laughter and radiant faces
All delighting in the magnificence of the day
The intense blue of the lake
The wispy white clouds floating overhead
The sun glistening off a myriad of boats
On the lake and below the bridge in the marina

Gratitude for all the beauty
That surrounds us everywhere
Whether we choose to see it or not
Is this the key to connect to Source?
It is for me: Gratitude and appreciation
Connects me to my Source of Being, anytime
Source is always here for me, for all of us

Source simply IS, never changing
Always here, always now, always IS

✢ ✢ ✢

Ancient Memories

When first we met
I felt an ancient memory astir
Deep within my breast
Was it in my heart? In my soul?
Or perhaps in my brain? My mind?
Unable to locate the source
Which seemed to be everywhere
Throughout my Being...
Remnants of an ancient memory?

Unaccustomed as I was
To such bewildering stirrings
Nestled deep within my every cell
I kept asking: WHO ARE YOU?
Why these vague memories?
Where did they come from?
Why do I need you?
I was in peace before we met
Before these remnants of an ancient memory

But slowly, more specific visions
Started crowding those memories
You were my lover
Ardent yet gentle
Still never a match for my own
Suddenly inflamed passions

But wait—you were not willing at all…
The lover—but an illusion?
Or the remnants of an ancient memory?

Then I recognized the parent in you
The parent figure I hardly knew
Scolding me for trespassing
Onto your soul territory
No ancient memories clouding YOUR Being
Stern and authoritarian
Harsh, merciless and unfeeling
When instead I needed understanding
With a pinch of tenderness

In your parent mode, unknowingly
You started calling me
By my short childhood name
Which I had not heard in years
Strange and familiar—how did you know?
A flash of ancient memory?
Oh how I needed a hug…
The parent—but an illusion?
Or remnants of an ancient memory?

Finally I reached for the friend
Perhaps—room for friendship?
Reluctant, tentative at best
You extended the odd kind word
Unsure, afraid of further trespasses

Busy, busy, always too busy
To allow ancient memories
To invade your consciousness
To meet remnants of MY ancient memory

How many pasts have we spent together
In different times, different places
Each playing the changing roles
Of lover, parent, child
And finally friend, perhaps
While at the moment of birth
The veil of forgetfulness so kindly
Or unkindly, perhaps
Wiped out all ancient memories

So that we could begin anew
The search for each other
And continue what started eons ago
Wondering if stirrings of
Some ancient memories would lead
Two strangers back to one another...
Are my senses so much keener than yours
To pick us these stirrings
Of persistent, ancient memories?

✣ ✣ ✣

A Layer Of Grief

It seems that I have grieved for years,
That buried deep inside of me,
Below my cheerful clown nature,
Below my inherently positive nature
There is this undefined layer of grief.

No matter how deep I go within
To find meaning in what is truthful
And to find real truth
In what is meaningful,
There is always this layer of grief.

No matter how I try to observe
The situation from a distance,
Not allowing my ready emotions
To forever cloud the issue,
There remains this constant layer of grief.

No matter how I try to see
Life through unbiased eyes,
To find new paths and options,
To remain a role model for many
And share my inner knowing…

When will I begin to understand and see
Grief as a blessing?

✝ ✝ ✝

I saw grief drinking a cup of sorrow and called out,
"It tastes sweet, does it not?"
"You've caught me," grief answered,
"and you've ruined my business:
How can I sell sorrow when you know it's a blessing?"

—Jalaluddin Rumi, 1207–1273

Sufi saint and Persian poet and mystic

Once Again

Once again we meet
By chance—or by design?

Not remembering the countless lives
We spent together in eternity
Loving, fighting, loving, learning
Each time leaving issues unresolved

Now back on this earth once again
To try once more—or not?
Will we finally deal with all those issues
Left unresolved from so many pasts?

Both loners in our own ways
Allowing but a precious few to glimpse into our souls
To protect our innermost values
And secrets never meant to be shared

Will one of us lack the courage
To face those unrealities—once again?
Or are we destined to visit some earth
Yet another time—once again?

If soul mates are indeed the ones
The difficult ones who can teach us the most
Then we are truly soul mates
With the most to learn from each other

Will we allow ourselves this time
To be each other's best teacher?
Or must we continue our apprenticeship
In yet another time and space –

Once Again?

✝ ✝ ✝

Reincarnation

Life makes very little sense
If we are just born, struggle painfully through life
And then die... To what higher purpose?

In the context of reincarnation, however,
Everything falls more meaningfully into place
And life begins to make more sense.

If we strive purposefully for inner fulfillment,
We consciously increase our awareness
For our soul to vibrate at ever higher frequencies.

Such evolution and refinement of the soul
Cannot be achieved in one single lifetime
But may take many, even countless, lifetimes.

"Déjà vu" of places, situations, or people
Is a common and frequent example
Of having lived other lives, elsewhere, with others.

Sometimes we meet people for the first time,
Yet feel that we have known them forever:
That is a glimpse into another lifetime.

In each lifetime we meet familiar souls
From some other lifetimes, elsewhere
With whom we still have outstanding issues.

Unless we deal with and resolve such issues
To further our spiritual growth and evolution,
We must keep returning again, and again

Until we have learned all our lessons
That we came to this earth to learn.
Until then, we must keep reincarnating...

✠ ✠ ✠

Choices

Sometimes I feel an inner sadness
Emanating from you across the distance

That in turn leaves me sad and helpless
Because you don't allow me to cheer you up

Because the only one allowed to help you
Is also the cause of your sadness

Because those are your choices
And you are responsible for them

As we all know, we must live by our choices
And deal with the consequences

Like it or not, you and I are still connected
Through the energy grid of this benevolent universe

✝ ✝ ✝

Leap Day

Who will be happier on Leap Day:
The women who have a legitimate chance today
To propose to the object of their affection?
Or the victims of such proposals who must decide
YES—or NO?

Surely, nervous anticipation must rule Leap Day.
Timid, or reluctant, or non-committal men
May try to evade the hunting female
Intent on finally capturing
Her elusive prey.

Or—is the burden of such a weighty step
On the anxious, hunting female?
Should she, or shouldn't she?
What if he laughs, or turns her down?
Brave—or foolish?

Would she prefer the man to take action?
Or impress him with her courage—or desperation?
Clearly, a two-edged sword…
Wait for him to ask—perhaps never –
Or wait another four years?

Thank goodness, I'm not in the running.
Would I prefer a man of action,
Or a timid one, waiting to be wooed?
No such burden on my shoulders any more…
I hope you find your own solution.

✝   ✝   ✝

Connected

Once upon a time so many moons ago
Two Indigo adults met quite by accident
In an obscure little place called Indigo

Setting in motion a curious chain
Of developments and emotional upheavals
That neither one had expected

That neither one understood
Or could possibly have foreseen
Now both are still groping in the dark

No doubt they are connected
Not romantically as one of them
Had so fervently hoped

But connected nevertheless
Perhaps they are slowly beginning to see
The outline of a purpose here

Only the Universe knows the reason
As for them—like it or not
Yes—they will always remain connected

✢ ✢ ✢

Soul Mates

On this earthly plane
We keep searching for our perfect soul mate
Which we know, or at least hope, exists.

It is a common belief that soul mates
Are those with whom we are so totally compatible
That rarely any need for discord arises.

But some claim that the opposite is true:
That our soul mates are those
Who challenge us the most and drive us crazy

Because growth and evolution
Develop from dealing successfully with challenges,
Not from comfortable complacency.

After all, ships are built to sail
And weather all manner of storms,
Not to stay safe and idle in the harbor.

Also, diamonds are formed by pressure -
And, are we not striving to be diamonds,
Pure and brilliant?

☩ ☩ ☩

Forget-You-Not

In vain I've tried to banish you from my thoughts
To exorcise you from my loving heart
To freeze you out of my suffering soul
But you are too deeply embedded in every fiber

In every cell of my sensuous Being
Locked in my cellular memory forever
Remaining in that unexplained connectedness
Across time and space

So I must keep writing, creating
Hoping to dull my pain
To un-create what destiny has so cruelly
Bestowed on me—or perhaps, on us?

But if we are indeed
The masters of our own thoughts
Then I must have brought this pain
This misery upon myself, to learn from

So that through suffering and experiencing fully
The bitter-sweet mysteries of this earthly life
I may cleanse and purify my soul
And learn to love unconditionally

But you, my beloved friend
Will remain always and forever
Across all time and space
My FORGET-YOU-NOT

‡ ‡ ‡

Enlightenment

I thought I had met a kindred fellow soul
On my path to enlightenment—
But I found only a mirage

I thought I had encountered sage Socrates
To learn from and exchange wisdom—
But I found only a phantom

Eagerly I had opened my mind and my heart
To learn and share and love—
But I found only indifference

Perhaps I was entranced by an illusionist—
How else could I see what was not there?
Is dis-illusion my great lesson?

In my quest for enlightenment
I found only mirages, phantoms, indifference—
Perhaps those were the enlightenment?

Perhaps The Quest
Is The Enlightenment?

✝ ✝ ✝

The Pedestal

Slim elegance of gleaming golden marble
Towering majestically in center space
Compelling a thousand yearning eyes
To admire the imposing statue atop
The pedestal

A figure of authority robed in black
Its piercing eyes demanding attention
Even obedience from its adoring subjects
Massing in eager anticipation around
The pedestal

"Emulate me!" his demeanor seems to urge
But his eyes remain cold and indifferent
He cannot communicate or be heard
Being just a silent but imposing statue atop
The pedestal

Disappointed, the masses slowly disperse
With an unwelcome new toughness in their hearts
Not having heard the longed-for mentoring wisdom
"He has nothing to say" they declare of the statue atop
The pedestal

Sad and abandoned, the imposing statue in black
Remains alone without the unconditional adoration
Of the thousand yearning eyes, being
No longer the expected mystic mentor atop
The pedestal

✦ ✦ ✦

Leave Me In Peace, Fantasy Lover

Finally he had banished her from his dreams
Forbidding her to enter his thoughts again
And yet—every once in a while
There she was, waiting for him once more

In brief waking moments between sleep times
She still tended to crop up unexpectedly
Suddenly, in his mind's default mode
NO! He screamed in self-defence: GET OUT!

Leave me alone! Give me back my peace!
If I cannot have you—don't torture me
You are so difficult to get rid of
Even with my most determined efforts!

Yet, this morning, there she was again
Waiting for him as he skipped down the stairs
Catching his hand before he could escape
Bringing it up to her lips, affectionately

How could he resist such an overture
No matter how uncharacteristic it was of her
So she started kissing his neck, his ears
Then moved to his lips—he did not withdraw

They were locked in tender, lingering embrace
"Oh, what heaven" he muttered softly in her ear
How long he had waited to bring her such heaven
How sad that they had missed so much time

Upon waking his dream did not yet end
He remained in the clutches of his captivating reverie
Leaving him with a wildly pounding heart
For the remainder of this precious day

My Forbidden, Beloved Fantasy
– Please Grant Me Peace –

✝ ✝ ✝

The Gatekeeper

Sometimes we fail to distinguish
Between loving, wanting, needing
And the choices may appear difficult

Listen to your gatekeeper

Loving is a blessing because it comes from the heart
Wanting ends in unhappiness because it comes from ego
Needing may be merely a cover for wanting

Listen to your gatekeeper

Whenever we don't get what we want
We will always get what we need
Because the wisdom of the universe will prevail

Trust your gatekeeper

Follow the gatekeeper's wise counsel
Listen to your whispering inner voice
Keep loving, and learn to love without wanting

✝ ✝ ✝

No Ring

During the recent magnificent full moon
Once again, as so many times before,
His past, unfulfilled love appeared in his dream
As if nothing had ever happened.

Sitting across from each other like old friends,
With many hurtful years of silence wiped out,
He suddenly noticed that her beautiful hands
Were now bare—no ring on any finger.

"What happened to the ring?" he asked her.
"Oh, we're no longer together," she replied simply.
He pondered that silently, with no further questions,
And he was surprised that it no longer mattered.

After all, she had never been available to him.
So why was he still thinking, dreaming of her
After years of painful detachment?
Would his unrequited love never leave him in peace?

✢ ✢ ✢

Poor Lolita

Life floats by, never missing a beat
While poor Lolita continues suckling
On a seductive but toxic lollypop
Given to her by a persuasive popinjay,
Trying to coax some sweetness out of it.

Spending months, even years of her life
Lollygagging in daydreamland,
Wishing and hoping and fantasizing
About an imagined mellow sweetness
That never materializes. Poor Lolita!

Until one day she awakens with a jolt,
With poison constricting her tender throat,
Her body struggling to win the upper hand
And all toxins finally oozing out of every pore,
Setting poor Lolita free, at last.

✝ ✝ ✝

Ode to a Fantasy Lover

(of Words)

Should your situation ever change
As situations sometimes
Have a tendency to do, and

Should you get your very own, well-earned
Two weeks, two/few weeks,
Too few weeks of freedom, and

Should you wonder/ponder
Where to take
Your Magical Self, and

Should you wonder/ponder
What other Self would be most Magical
For you at that time:

Let my Self whisk you away
To the Magical Kingdom of nowhere,
No-w-here, now here

Just our two Magical Selves in now here
To find out if two Selves
Can meld into

TwoSelves, for a while at least,
Rediscovering those fiery passions
Of younger years

Two fantasy lovers in the Magical Kingdom
Of nowhere,
No-w-here, now here

✝ ✝ ✝

Inspired Perspectives

A Clown's Perspective

Self-confidence is not being afraid to occasionally make a fool of yourself—it is part of being able to laugh at yourself. Don't take yourself so seriously: no one else does. Cultivate a keen sense of the absurd.

As long as you are in the company of yourself, you should never be bored, because being bored would be an insult to yourself.

Love your essence: your physical body is the way your essence can have presence in this world. Your body is the temporary home for your eternal soul. Therefore, cultivate and be happy with who you are inside.

In this world there are givers and there are takers, and I am a giver. However, that does not ever guarantee any reciprocation.

Quiet people who don't say much are not always still waters that run deep. Sometimes they are simply monumental bores with nothing to say, with rarely an opinion on anything.

The right attitude creates the capacity to enjoy and appreciate what we have, which in turn brings contentment and happiness into our life. You have a choice: You control your attitude, or it controls you.

If you don't like losing, then stop the ongoing war with yourself. This means that you should make peace with your past so it won't keep spoiling your present.

Be careful to never give yourself enough rope to allow others to witness your own self-hanging.

Pain is inevitable, but suffering is optional. Why? Because pain is physical, while suffering is a state of mind, an attitude—and you control your attitude.

When in doubt, err on the side of having a life. When you have to choose between two evils, choose the one you haven't tried before.

Love is a choice and, clown that I am, I always choose love. If you are not loving, others may also find it difficult to love you.

Don't fall victim to the incurable foot-in-mouth disease.

Nothing is ever as bad as it seems, because just two days from now, tomorrow will be yesterday. And yesterday wasn't so bad, was it?

In case you are schizophrenic, you will at least always have each other.

People may forget what you said or what you did, but people will never forget how you made them feel. That's why a good clown will always try to make people feel happy. Keep smiling at people and let them wonder what you're up to.

The time to be eccentric is NOW! What other people think of you is none of your business. Take Funky Lily's word for it.

Be sure to treat yourself regularly to mind candy and soul food.

✝ ✝ ✝

"Growing old is mandatory.
Growing up is optional."

—Anon

The World of Illusion

There must be very few people over 30 who have never seen those 3-D pictures in the newspapers or 3-D posters exhibited in malls around the city. You know the ones: the flat, indecipherable pictures full of small, busy detail, often leaves or flowers or weave-like patterns. Were you ever able to penetrate that world of illusions?

Well-meaning friends had given me what they considered useful pointers. "Just keep staring at it until your eyes get blurry," one said. "No—no, bring the picture right up to your nose and focus on it, then pull it back," another instructed. "You have to figure out your own way of seeing it—everybody is different," a third one proposed.

Well, a few headaches later, I decided to give my poor, blurred, strained eyes a rest and file those newspaper clippings under "Miscellaneous: Unfinished Business." I had failed miserably and was debating whether I should feel inadequate or just forget about the whole thing. I decided on the latter.

Then, one day, I found myself in a large mall, roaming around aimlessly while waiting for my one-hour glasses. Oh yes, I needed stronger eyeglasses; could those 3-D pictures have anything to do with that? Anyway, I suddenly found myself confronted with an entire exhibit of such 3-D posters, also called pixelgrams, or stereograms, or magic eye, of varying sizes. My curiosity got the better of me and I started my process of staring and sighing in frustration.

"Do you know how to look at them?" a young saleslady asked me mercifully. "Let me show you." She guided me to a large, busy poster, full of nonsensical dots and curls and lines and stars.

"Can you see your reflection in the glass? Yes? Just look into your own eyes in the reflection. Stare at them without blinking. Then you'll see the picture."

I stood there, staring into my own eyes, waiting for whatever, trying desperately not to blink. Suddenly, my reflection disappeared. The front of the poster disappeared; there was now only a clear pane of glass. Deep behind that glass, a picture materialized in three dimensions. I couldn't believe my eyes! I was transported into another world, a magical, secret world that only the initiated could see. How thrilling!

First, I saw a snake. What was that snake doing there? No—it was not a snake but a cable, leading to a man with a giant helmet covering his entire head. Oh, a diver! There was a large mass behind and below him. That must be a sunken ship, I thought. I blinked, and the scene disappeared: I was back at the flat nonsense with the dots and curls and lines and stars.

I took a deep breath and blinked a few times to relieve the eyestrain. Then I started focusing on my reflection again, and in no time the 3-D image reappeared. Once back inside this world of illusion, I allowed my eyes to roam around.

Soon I found the diver with his old-fashioned giant diving helmet and his cable—but wait!—no, this was not a diver but an astronaut, with the helmet being part of his space suit. The cable was his umbilical cord to the space ship, and the large mass behind and below him was a planet, perhaps the earth. Continuing my visual exploration I discovered other, smaller heavenly bodies floating around in this magical space. Wow!

I exited the picture, giving my eyes a rest and reflecting on what I had just experienced. Unbelievable! With a trick of the eye, I had left the busy mall and entered the silent, wondrous world of space. I was so thrilled that I impatiently moved to other posters to discover and explore their silent, magical worlds.

I encountered dusty animals in the desert; a magnificent eagle hovering over his nest high atop a tree in the mountains; two boxers fighting in the ring; a colony of penguins. Looking past a golfer on the green, I could follow the trees lining the golf course for what seemed a mile.

In my total astonishment I would emit childlike sounds of wonderment and delight that caused other people to turn and stare at me. 'Really—at her age' I could read in their faces.

One smaller laminated poster, titled The Return, in beautiful rose-purple-mauve colors, captured my imagination enough to buy it. A perfect surprise gift for my husband! No doubt it would stimulate his scientific mind to probe how all this could possibly be done. Besides, it would always make an interesting conversation piece.

"The idea is to focus your vision on your reflection, which means behind the front image," I explained to him. "As long as your focus remains behind the front, you can explore the image as much as you want. But as soon as you change focus, the image disappears, and you're back to the flat picture."

My husband was intrigued, and he explored it for a long time, seeing more details as he became more experienced. "Isn't it thrilling?" I asked. "I still can't get over accessing a whole new world like this!"

"Yes, I find it thrilling, too, but for very different reasons," he finally said. "Philosophical reasons. Just think: what you see is not what there is. If we accept a picture like this at face value, there is not much to see, and we can dismiss it easily. But if we take the trouble to look behind the flat front…"

"Just like with people," I burst out. "If we don't bother looking behind the façade, we may never find out what's behind it, good or bad…"

We both kept exploring The Return which depicts a dove in flight, carrying an olive branch, and philosophizing about the world of illusion and reality, only briefly wondering why the dove was not the traditional white but a mauve-purple.

It took the visit of a friend to add yet another dimension. "The Return?" she asked. "A dove in flight, carrying an olive branch? Why—that's the biblical dove flying back to Noah's ark after the great flood!"

Reflecting on that later on, I dared speculate further. Of course, the world had lost its white innocence a long time ago. But there is, in fact, a resurgence of spirituality everywhere, and that spirituality is reflected in the colors mauve and purple. So, with seemingly increasing violence in many parts of the world, is this purple dove a symbol of hope, returning to a new, more spiritual world?

Or am I lost in yet another world of illusion?

Even now, years later, my husband stops regularly on the way out the door to contemplate the dove in flight behind the flat, indecipherable front, to remind himself to always look deeper, because nothing is as it seems.

✛ ✛ ✛

Remember When?

Are we getting old if we remember:

… when men used to wear tattoos, and women earrings? Nowadays, it seems that the average man under 35 will sport at least one earring, and many young women will display a tattoo somewhere on their body, whether immediately visible or not…

… when women wore long hair, and men short? Is it terribly old-fashioned to still consider hair a woman's crowning glory? Somehow, men got hold of that old guideline and made it their own, while many women now cut their hair short enough to need to shave their necks…

… when young women used to blush when they were embarrassed? Well, that's not cool anymore. Now, they are embarrassed when they blush, because they might actually have shown some true emotions…

… when 'GAY' meant merry, lively, light-hearted, bright, happy, joyous, etc.? Actually, all these definitions are still in the dictionary, but you don't dare use them in those contexts any more. Nowadays, GAY strictly denotes a certain sexual preference…

… when closets were used for hanging or storing clothes and other items? Nowadays, they are a hiding place for certain people to come out of…

… when the only people who wore black were mourners, old folks, and members of certain underground organizations, while young people enjoyed more colorful clothes? Now, many young and not so young men and women have an all-black wardrobe, like a new uniform. Of course, this eliminates the daily dilemma of what to wear: everything coordinates beautifully with everything else. Besides, there is much less laundry to do, as black doesn't show dirt as much. Or—perhaps they ARE mourning something…

… when grass was mowed, not smoked? And when Coke was a drink to quench your thirst, not a drug to fry your brain?

… when amber traffic lights meant slowing down, getting ready to stop the car? Today, somehow, they seem more like a license to speed up to make it through the red light before the cars from the other side threaten to crunch your vehicle into an accordion…

Do we mind getting old enough to remember these things? And when the day comes when nobody remembers any more, will it matter?

✛ ✛ ✛

A Case for Reincarnation

Life makes no sense at all if we are just born, struggle through life, and then die… what for? To what higher purpose?

That's why, after years of thought and searching, I decided that the only way life would make any sense was in the context of reincarnation. Since then, everything has managed to fall into place in a purposeful way.

I believe in reincarnation because I believe in the evolution of the soul. There is just no way that a soul can evolve and purify in a single lifetime. At best, it would take many, many lifetimes! Only after many lifetimes of consciously increasing our awareness and purposefully striving for inner fulfillment can our soul evolve to ever higher levels, to vibrate at ever higher frequencies.

Most of us have experienced "déjà vu" in places, or situations, or even with people. I have met people I felt I had known for a long time, even having just met them for the first time. I believe that we keep meeting souls from other lifetimes with whom we still have outstanding issues to resolve—usually people who give us a hard time and always push our buttons, and vice versa.

These things are not easy to deal with, especially since we don't remember any of our other lives; we may only get glimpses here and there, in such "déjà vu's." If we don't deal with these situations and thus further our spiritual growth, we have to keep coming back to face such situations and such people again, and again, until we've learned all our lessons.

For example: I'm sure that I will keep meeting my mother a few more times in future lives in different roles and situations—after all, I 'fled' to Canada to get away from her, as far away as possible. At the time I was not aware of such issues and options, and although we made peace just before she passed on, nothing was discussed. But I feel that we did make some progress, because for the first time in my life she showed me some affection a week before she died in the late 1980s.

It is a common belief that soul mates are people with whom we are so totally compatible that there is rarely any discord. But Dr. Wayne Dyer, the internationally known author of many books and speaker in the field of self-development and spiritual growth, proposes the opposite: that our soul mates are those who challenge us the most. He bases this belief on the experiences with some of his children who constantly push his buttons. He feels that they are the ones most responsible for his constant growth and evolution and creativity.

This makes a lot of sense, because we don't learn that much from the people we're never conflicted with, although they do make life a lot easier.

But ships aren't built to stay safe in the harbor: they are built to sail and weather storms. Others have said, "Diamonds are formed by pressure"… and, are we not striving to be diamonds, pure and brilliant?

✛ ✛ ✛

Detachment

The Eastern philosophy discipline of detachment has been an ongoing struggle for me for decades. Initially, my concept of detachment was non-involvement: so how could one get emotionally involved and remain detached? Although I've come a long way since my earliest exposure to that difficult concept through yoga, I'm regularly given the opportunity to examine my progress so far. Sometimes I win, sometimes I lose.

I have made great strides in trying to enjoy people and things without being attached to them, yet without becoming jaded, or taking anybody or anything for granted. However, sometimes in my exuberance of meeting new people to love, I'm still prone to getting attached, and I'm working on that. Although I now come with no strings attached most of the time, my ultimate aim is to love unconditionally, and that's a tall order.

What has been fun, however, was getting detached from myself. Once you are past fifty, and you've put in your years getting your priorities in order and discovering and developing your spirituality, along with accepting both your strengths and weaknesses, you begin to feel comfortable with yourself. After all, self-acceptance is part of your self-esteem. Now you don't have to compete anymore, because you know your own worth.

That's when you get to the point of watching yourself from a comfortable distance, observing your foibles and successes, without any guilt or shame or judgment or false pride, without being hard on yourself. As the Desiderata suggests: "Beyond a wholesome discipline, be gentle with yourself…"

Life takes on a different dimension; you realize what is important, and what is not. Other people can no longer diminish your self-worth, or upset your life balance. You have become responsible for both your actions and reactions, and you accept responsibility for and the consequences of your choices, because you are now making conscious choices.

This kind of detachment was very helpful when I was suddenly diagnosed with a large, possibly cancerous, pelvic mass. Instead of panicking, I became an observer. I reminded myself that I am not my body, but that I am simply the temporary custodian of my body which is just part of ME, my essence—a part that needed fixing if it was to last until I was ready to leave this planet, the same way a car needs servicing and fixing when necessary to keep it in good running order.

This detached attitude got me through all the various tests and CT scans and unpleasant Barium intrusions, without fear or panic. It got me through recovering from the cold I caught from lying in the freezing operating room, half naked, for whatever length of time; from the grotesquely swollen upper lip that was cut and damaged when they inserted (or removed) the standard-procedure oxygen tube to my mouth; from the post-operative elephantine grace after my body was adorned with a 7 ½ inches long masterpiece of body piercing, 20 tiny staples lined up in a fairly straight line, keeping it all together until it healed on its own.

I was able to laugh at it all because it was not personal. The fact that my operation took place Friday the 13th was funny because my surgeon was Chinese, and Friday the 13th has no significance for the Chinese, and I'm not superstitious.

My attitude remained positive and cheerful throughout; I felt no pain, no noticeable lack of energy. After two days, my doctor looked at me and declared, "You look far too healthy to lie around in a hospital bed. Go home! You can leave tomorrow morning."

In the meantime, the staples have been removed, but the healing will continue for another few weeks. Although the cancerous growth has been excised, I will still need a follow-up in a cancer clinic to make sure that no further cancer is lurking anywhere in my body; until then, I will not be out of the woods.

While the standard rule is that one cannot drive a car for 3-4 weeks after surgery, I was driving again within 10 days, with the doctor's consent. Unfortunately, gym and ballroom dancing would have to wait a little longer! But my detachment allowed me to follow my recovery from an observer's perspective, always applying common sense and logic to any situation.

I feel that my grasp of detachment, such as it is, has served me in ways I never realized it could. It has allowed me, so far, to recover more quickly than average, to be grateful for all the new experiences, and to appreciate life and the caring people around me even more.

2002

✝ ✝ ✝

Anatomy of Pleasure

Or: Putting Things into Context

Ah, pleasure! The very word conjures up exhilarating expectation in my soul. Does it in yours? I hope it does, because in today's depressing economic climate when many of us don't have much to cheer about, we should make an effort to recognize and enjoy little every-day pleasures and put things into context.

Pleasure, however, is such a totally subjective concept that each of us may have a different idea of what it is. According to the dictionary, pleasure ranges from ecstasy to a simple opposite of pain. But, generally, it is gratification of the senses or of the mind; excitement, relish or happiness produced by enjoyment or even the expectation of enjoyment; agreeable sensation or emotions, such as satisfaction and delight.

To a homeless and hungry person, finding part of an uneaten sandwich in a garbage bin can likely provide more pleasure than a yacht trip does to a millionaire. If there were a scientific way of evaluating pleasure with an instrument that could accurately measure and record biological changes that take place in the body and the mind and assign some numerical value to the level of pleasure experienced by the individual, it would indeed be interesting to compare the pleasure of the hungry person to that of the millionaire.

Any bets? The discarded sandwich produces excitement, happiness and ultimately gratification of the senses. The yacht trip, based on my own observation, produced pleasure only to the extent that guests on board were willing to admire the yacht and the owner. (I deprived the owner of that pleasure by daring to be preoccupied with my queasy stomach. Unforgivable!)

In other words, these two types of pleasure stem from totally different motivations. The homeless person's happiness is the result of having a REAL need at least partly fulfilled, while the yachting pleasure may be based solely on the PERCEIVED need to impress other people. (Perhaps I'm unfairly generalizing as I personally know only one millionaire, so far.)

On another front, it is quite conceivable that a teenager shattering his eardrums with mind-numbing rock music will experience the same level of ecstasy as a classical music devotee listening to Albinoni's soul-soothing Adagio, or a jazz fan 'deliriating' over the inimitable piano stylings of Oscar Peterson. Our millionaire friend is perfectly satisfied with dawn-to-dusk elevator music piped in through proudly displayed speakers built into every ceiling of his impressive mansion.

One can no more argue about pleasure-producing taste in music—or arts, or sports, or anything else—than one can unequivocally state that a chef's seafood crepe masterpiece provides a higher level of gratification or sensual delight than a sinfully rich chocolate truffle cake. The music lovers experience gratification of the senses and of the mind listening to their favorite music, while the millionaire may, once again, base his pleasure on the perceived admiration by his guests.

This raises a question: Does the time it takes to access pleasure add to or diminish the experience of pleasure? A music lover can start listening to a favorite recording, or play an instrument, practically anytime or anywhere; there is almost instant access to pleasure. Singing, even for the most self-conscious, is as accessible as the nearest shower. On the other hand, a sailing or flying enthusiast must endure hours, days, or evens seasons of waiting or preparing to access the pleasure of sailing the waters or the skies.

Is it preferable to have easy or instant access to pleasure, and thus relieve stress more rapidly and efficiently? Or does the waiting and preparing enhance and increase the gratification of the result, such as a vacation after months of planning? Do devotees of hard-to-access pleasures find gratification in the waiting and preparing? One would imagine, however, that they must also be able to access instant pleasures in order to relieve stress more immediately, the way a cup of instant soup relieves hunger pangs immediately.

Luckily, pleasure is not limited to any class of people or any level of affluence. The most conscientious ascetic finds a certain pleasure in his rigorous self-denial, while the devoted hedonist must continuously probe ever further afield to find gratification for his jaded soul. The low-income family enjoys a no-cost walk in the park much more than the millionaire who worries about the considerable fuel cost for even a short yacht trip. A poor child living in the slums may have as much pleasure playing with sticks and stones as the millionaire's child trying to figure out the most expensive electronic wizardry.

Therein lies a delightful, gratifying justice.

In the end, it all boils down to appreciating the little things in life, from a charming smile flashed your way, to a job well done, to the forecast rain holding off until you get home when you forgot to take your umbrella.

It also helps to develop and maintain a sense of humor and a positive attitude toward life in general. For example: You will appreciate your overall good health much more and gripe about an occasional headache much less if you remember that the French once had an effective and permanent solution for a headache: the guillotine.

Ah, the pleasure of putting things into context!

✦ ✦ ✦

"A sense of humour is just common sense dancing."

—Anon

Purpose of Life: A Theory

At some point in our life, we all think about why we are here, trying to find a purpose for being on this earth. Surely our cave-dwelling ancestors must have already pondered such questions, wondering whether there might not be something more to existence than hunting and surviving, maybe scribbling some drawings on the cave wall, then dying young.

Over the millenia, countless theories must have surfaced, many rivalling each other. Humans developed and refined their thinking capacities, and many religions were created, many with their own God, each producing yet more theories. As nobody ever came back after death to truly enlighten us, we are still groping for something that makes sense.

Most people try and live an honourable life, become responsible and loving parents, and strive to be upstanding citizens. Whether or not that was their main purpose in life, or whether something greater was expected of them but unknowingly not fulfilled, is hard to know. While some people realize their purpose very early in life, many others start looking within only once they reach a certain maturity, and still others never question at all.

However, when certain people die, be they ordinary neighbours or well-known personalities, we may get a glimpse of perhaps a higher purpose. That's when we realize that even death can serve a purpose. It seems that many of us have to experience painfully low points in our life before we can produce another major spurt of spiritual growth, or to find our true purpose. Instead of asking 'Why Me?' and wallowing in self-pity, or fearfully shying away from a daunting new task, we should ask, 'How can I turn this into something positive and make the best of it?'

Just following everyday news, we realize that untimely death or other life-changing events or challenges can fulfill an unforeseen purpose. Here is my own theory, with just a few examples to back it up.

✝

When actor Christopher Reeve, better known as Superman, finally died after lengthy and partly successful rehabilitation following his devastating riding accident that left him paralyzed, the world was shocked and saddened. He had been at the top of his game, a successful celebrity and happy family man - he had it all. Then he seemed to have lost it all in the tragic accident that left him suicidal, until he realized that his loving family still needed him.

As he was rich enough to hire the very best rehabilitation professionals who managed to get him to sit in a chair and talk with a tube in his throat, he set himself a goal to raise awareness of spinal cord injuries and lobby Washington. Because of his high profile, he succeeded in raising huge amounts of money for research into such injuries before he died.

In other words, it seems that he only realized his true purpose in life once he had lost everything he had had before. Without the accident, he would have continued his successful and glamorous life and would never have fulfilled his true purpose.

The tragedy of his paralysis was needed to trigger the beginning of the fulfillment of his ultimate purpose in life.

✝

In a more recent case, the tragic death of 15-year-old Brandon also made world-wide news and raised all sorts of questions.

Brandon had wanted to keep playing hockey, but he could not advance beyond house league because he was considered too small. Always having been a small child, he was still just 5'3" at age 15—an age where a boy wants to look and feel big, and not still look like a child. He had to give up his beloved hockey, and he was angry.

He found fulfillment in online gaming. He became so deeply involved in playing his Xbox gaming console that he became totally addicted—what is called pathological gambling—and his personality underwent a negative change. When his parents could not break his obsession with gaming, they felt they had no choice but to take away his Xbox. That's when Brandon ran away from home and, after extensive search efforts by police officers and search dogs, helicopters and volunteers, his body was finally found by local deer hunters in a wooded area about three weeks later. It seems that he died of chest injuries he suffered from falling out of a tree.

The devastated family, in trying to turn this tragedy into a positive legacy, has established a foundation to facilitate underprivileged and undersized children to participate in sports activities, feeling that no child should be barred from playing sports, and thus be driven to negative activities and behaviour. Brandon's untimely and needless death seemed to point the parents towards their purpose in life.

One could even speculate that, unbeknownst to himself, it was Brandon's ultimate purpose in life to follow his self-destructive route in order to allow his parents to start effecting change for an ever-growing modern-day problem.

✢

In yet another recent case, the needless death of a high-profile Broadway and film actress might also bring about much-needed change. Natasha was in her prime both personally and professionally, with an impeccable pedigree as part of a prominent British acting dynasty, and with a happy and fulfilled personal life.

While her well-known actor husband was working on a film in Toronto, Natasha decided to spend some time in Quebec learning to ski. On a beginner's hill with a private instructor, in beautiful weather, she fell innocently in the fresh and soft snow, bumped her head and walked away.

It was only later back at the hotel that she got a violent headache and, with a few unfortunate detours, was rushed to different hospitals where she quickly died. She had not been wearing a ski helmet, and it seems that it is common that a bump on the head can lead to swelling of the brain, resulting in severe headaches some time later, and often in death.

Although there were 138 hospitalizations in one year in Canada alone due to head injuries from skiing and snowboarding accidents, it took this high-profile death to create world-wide attention and to re-ignite debates on the need for ski helmets. As half of the deaths on ski slopes due to head injuries are the result of people not wearing ski helmets, the issue of mandatory use versus personal choice has once again become a hot topic. While the USA and Europe have helmet regulations, Canada has still not seriously addressed the problem.

It seems that, once again, it took the tragic death of a famous person to raise awareness of an issue and to highlight the need for more education. Although Natasha's unexpected early death plunged her family into deep shock and suffering, perhaps this was her ultimate purpose in life, unbeknownst to even herself.

✞

Then, on a more uplifting note and having nothing to do with death, there was Susan, the unemployed, middle-aged virgin from the Scottish hinterlands who became an instant singing star on the popular *Britain's Got Talent* show. Large and heavy, and looking frumpy and unglamorous in her plain dress, with huge, never-plucked eyebrows and no make-up, Susan had a condescending and snickering audience gasping and cheering within seconds after opening her mouth to sing. Her wonderful voice instantly elevated her from a talent show joke to the latest U-Tube superstar within a day.

How far Susan's instant world-wide success will take her is irrelevant. The interesting fallout from her stage appearance was that she motivated and inspired hundreds, if not thousands of other middle-aged women around the world to reassess their own personal situation and finally start living their own dream. Some got up the courage to go back to school and get that degree they had always wanted. Others gave up an unfulfilling job to start their own business, or get involved with world peace or environmental causes.

When Susan decided to follow her dream of singing after her mother died, she took the risk of going against the normal superficial expectations of youth and beauty and body image, proving that one truly cannot judge a book by its cover. Nothing could intimidate or discourage her.

In the process, and probably without realizing it, she started on her surprising purpose in life, becoming a role model and unlikely poster matron for all those women who had lost faith, but who were now willing to take risks to pursue their own dream.

✝

As we never see the whole picture of life but only fragments of it, who are we to question the reasons behind any tragedy, perceived injustice, or life-changing event or challenge?

If we would start viewing such events from the angle of purpose, we could learn to look at life very differently.

✝ ✝ ✝

A Spiritual Orgasm

She woke up with a start, her heart pounding and her pulse racing. Sitting up in bed, she felt the exhilaration rush through her body like a continuous wave. It was only 4:31 AM; plenty of time to reflect on what was happening to her before it was time to get up.

Was it a dream that had unleashed this emotional intoxication? She searched her mind for some remnants of a dream, tried to regress herself into the last dream state, but could not. She found nothing.

No—it was not a dream, but a revelation, she suddenly realized. The word BONDING hit her on the forehead with a jolt, smack between the eyes, knocking her back onto the pillow. Of course—she had bonded! That's what was so exciting!

BONDED! She did not bond very often, being a reserved and private person. In her adult life, she could likely count her bondings on one hand, and in her childhood it probably never happened at all…

She tried to sort out her various relationships from her bondings. One of her few regrets in life was that she had never bonded with her mother, except perhaps—maybe—a little, a few days before her mother died when they made peace after a life of friction caused by two hard heads confronting each other on every issue. Her father had died when she was very young, and she had hardly known him. Even her only sister remained rather a stranger after all these years, a result of a family torn apart.

She had several good, dear friends, but not what she would call bonding quality. Yes, she and her girlfriend in the USA had bonded instantly when they met one weekend at a Yoga retreat many years ago, and they were still surrogate sisters to this date. She had also bonded with a young man back in her young and foolish days—soul mates, they called each other, although she had declined to marry him. And she had most definitely bonded with one of her older cousins far away, and with a schoolmate—another surrogate sister. She kept in touch with them all, and no matter how long they didn't see each other, no time at all passed between visits or phone calls.

And now she had bonded again. How did it happen? What made bonding happen?

She had known this man only for a very short time, and they met professionally on a regular basis. But whenever they spent time together, they grew closer, without either of them intending it. She had felt awkward about that, as if two adult professionals were not supposed to grow closer. Also, she was afraid that it might be a schoolgirl crush and that she would appear foolish.

But bonding was somehow liberating… she didn't really know how or why, but it was exciting! It seemed to give her the freedom to clarify her feelings; she knew where she herself stood. It was alright to have feelings beyond admiration and respect and strong liking for another person, and age somehow didn't enter into it at all.

There was an unconditionality about bonding, a letting go. Rules did not apply. Certain inhibitions were removed. Maybe that was the difference between friendship and bonding, between just chemistry and bonding: the unconditionality of it all.

Elated with the results of her reflections, she fell back asleep again.

✢

To her surprise, she found herself dreaming about him a few days later. The bonding seemed to have deepened her feelings for him, propelling her relationship with him onto a different level. She decided to write down her bonding experience and send him a copy, wondering how he would react to her boldness.

About a week later he called on a business matter and mentioned her writing, almost in passing, at the end of their conversation. She was disappointed that he found it only 'nice' and 'touching'—but at least he did not seem upset. Probably he didn't quite know what to make of it…

Their relationship did not change perceptively; their fondness for each other never progressed openly beyond a warm and lingering hug at the end of their sessions together.

Why did it come as such a shock to her to finally realize that he was not interested in her as a woman? She was clearly more to him than just a client. She tended to get lost in his hugs, hardly able to repress her strong feelings, and she didn't know how to handle his seemingly mixed signals.

Her dreams became wilder and more creative, with him as a willing and passionate participant. She was actually quite puzzled by the whole thing, because he was not her type at all. His face indicated a rather freewheeling past, and that had never appealed to her in a man. But she realized that the past was of no importance because the present was the only reality, and she liked the way he was now.

So she had allowed herself to be seduced by his maturity, his natural intelligence, his unpretentiousness, his way of listening, his endearing straightforwardness, his voice. That combination was a deadly turn-on for her, and her hormones had been running amok for weeks now.

One day she decided to discuss her feelings openly with him, to find out where he stood, if anywhere. He was very sympathetic and seemingly understanding, but he made it very clear that he did not intend to take their relationship any further, and their session ended with the usual warm, lingering hug.

The unconditionality of her bonding with him was put to a severe test: if she decided to continue her feelings for him—as if she had any choice!—there were to be no conditions on her part. Devastated as she was, her dreams grew more intense but changed focus entirely. It became increasingly difficult for her to separate her night dreams from her semi-conscious twilight dreams. Instead of unrestricted passion, they now spent hours together just talking and exploring each other's mind and innermost feelings and concerns and aspirations. They marveled at the similarities of their European backgrounds, their insecurities and personal patterns of self-discipline and defense mechanisms; how both had to start working and earn a living at an early age at the expense of schooling, and how both had managed to acquire some higher education later in life and make something of themselves, against the odds; how both had the courage to show their respective vulnerabilities, at least to each other.

In those dreams, they both felt that they could become soul mates—in fact, she felt that she already was. After all, each was both student and teacher to the other already. But, she wondered, were those wonderful gifts such as bonding and soul-mating always reciprocal? Or could they remain one-sided and, therefore, incomplete? One partner missing out on the soul-fulfillment of it all? She didn't know, and there was no one she felt free to ask, not even her Swami at the yoga retreat.

Over the countless hours of dreamtime together, he began to realize that her bonding with him was his guarantee that he never needed to feel insecure or threatened in her presence—that her motivation was always based on unconditional love. And he began to blossom, and the worry frown between his eyes began to disappear.

How she loved those dreams! Unrealistic probably/possibly, but so wonderful and soothing, and in many ways more fulfilling than the passionate and exciting fantasy love-making—which she missed, of course. She felt closer to him now than ever, but she never told him. She was not ready for another rejection.

✢

In the meantime, she continued her daily yoga routines, spending weekends at the yoga retreat. She tried to practice the ever so difficult principle of detachment, without great success. Even her meditations seemed to work against her in that effort.

While contemplating life in her private, sacred place during one of her meditations, she suddenly saw him there. How did he get there? Nobody knew of this place that existed only in her mind.

But there he was, among the tall sunflowers, looking at her silently, waiting. Finally, he moved toward her and took her left hand into his right and, holding hands, they walked slowly and silently through this enchanting field of sunflowers.

They communicated with each other without ever saying a word, focusing on their goals in life, wondering what direction their relationship would take, imagining the circumstances that would allow them to make the right decisions, and to find fulfillment with the right life partner.

Throughout this entire journey they never let go of each other. Slowly she felt his hand melding with hers until there was only one hand. Two arms ending up in one hand, and it was perfectly natural. As their communication progressed, the two arms melded into each other, so that their bodies were touching, and their two shoulders became one.

At the end of the field there was a small, clear pond where the water was always warm and caressing, and where she had often spent time just enjoying the warm sunshine and the lovely breeze.

As they arrived at the pond, they bent down to look at their reflections in the clear water, and they both watched as their bodies now melded totally into each other. His body disappeared inside hers; he became part of her.

Essentially, she now saw just her own body and her own face, although she could see his blue eyes inside her own blue eyes. But now there was a bottomless depth to her eyes that hadn't been there before. And that sparkle: was it in the water, or in her eyes?

It had all been such a natural process as if there were no other way of Being. She was in an absolute state of ecstasy as she moved back through the sunflowers, alone now, but feeling exquisitely complete and fulfilled. Her heart was full to bursting and her soul seemed to expand into the vastness of eternity.

Nothing like that had ever happened to her before, but she was neither surprised nor shocked. Coming out of her meditation, she walked over to a mirror and looked into her own eyes, wondering if or how her life would be different now.

Had this been just a normal progression from bonding to melding? In this state, how high could she soar? Could this be called a spiritual orgasm?

It didn't really matter. Once again, she didn't know the answer, but it seemed such a natural state of Being that she wanted it to go on forever, regardless of the reality she had to face at her next meeting with him.

✣ ✣ ✣

A Legend Relived

Once upon a time, in about 750 AD, there lived a lovely maiden by the name of Genoveva, who was the daughter of the Duke of Brabant, so she was also known as Genoveva of Brabant.

Shortly after she married Count Siegfried of Trier, her husband had to go off to battle, and he appointed his butler Golo to look after his wife during his absence. When Golo started making advances to the pregnant Genoveva and she refused him, Golo threw her into the dungeon where she gave birth to Siegfried's son, whom she called Schmerzensreich—or Sorrowful—because of all the pain and sorrow she had to endure.

When Siegfried returned from battle, Golo accused Genoveva of adultery, so Siegfried ordered his wife killed. However, her executioners took pity on her and helped her escape into the forest. There she found a cave where she and the boy could hide, and she continued living in that forest with her little son for seven years, sharing their space with deer and getting nourishment from them.

One day, when Siegfried was in the forest hunting deer, to his great surprise he discovered Genoveva, looking a bit wild from her years of living in the forest but still lovely, and for the first time he also met his son, Schmerzensreich. Learning the truth behind Golo's accusation, he asked her for forgiveness, and he brought both of them back to the castle. Although Genoveva had forgiven Golo, the husband ordered him to be executed for his betrayal. Later, when Genoveva died, Siegfried became a hermit, and his son Schmerzensreich stayed with him.

✥

Over the centuries, this legend of Genoveva, or Genevieve, as a chaste and loving but falsely accused and repudiated wife, has made its way into the folklore of many countries: Germany, Switzerland, France, England, Scotland, and Scandinavia, and into many theatre productions. It seems that Robert Schumann based his only opera *Genoveva* on such a tale, and that Puccini's opera *Suor Angelica* as well as Offenbach's *Genevieve de Brabant* are also based on the same legend.

Although most likely a fictitious story, a supposed Genoveva cave in Germany is still being visited, no longer by hermits and refugees, or hunters and herdsmen, but by curious hikers who can rest their weary bones on benches along the wall of the cave, using the steps cut into the rock.

One theatre performance of "Genoveva and Schmerzensreich" took place in a Catholic boarding school, called Theresianum, for girls at the High School level. A few stone throws away, just down the hill, was the boarding school for girls in the lower grades. That's where Mollina Tarin spent several years until Molly was moved to a foster family elsewhere in the country in the middle of Grade 5.

Given that there were no boys available anywhere in the vicinity, and that Molly was the smallest girl in the boarding school, she was chosen to play Genoveva's son, six-year-old Schmerzensreich, although she was really eight. Molly was blonde and blue-eyed, just like the Germanic Schmerzensreich was reported to be, and in her make-shift deer skin clothes and bare feet she would easily pass as a boy.

On the day of the performance, the nuns excitedly spent a few hours getting Molly ready, curling her shoulder-length hair to make it appear shorter and more boyish. "Oh, what a cute little boy you are," they cooed and fussed. Molly, a naturally shy girl, was both flattered and confused, not sure whether she really wanted to be a boy. She remembered when, in a previous cold winter, she was singing on the radio with her kindergarten class, wearing a knitted woollen tuque with all her hair tucked under it, and somebody called her a boy. Outraged, she had pulled off her tuque to allow her lovely golden locks to spill down to her shoulders, stamped her foot and said defiantly, "I'm a GIRL!" Perhaps an early display of feminism? But now, to be on stage with grown-ups, the only child in such a grand play, was too exciting to worry about looking like a boy.

Her role was very simple, without any speaking parts. The other actors, all high school girls, seemed very tall and mature, just like grown-ups. But then she, Molly, was so little, that on her First Communion earlier that same year, her chin couldn't reach the top of the ledge to receive Holy Communion, and she needed a pillow under her knees to raise her up. Therefore, almost everybody seemed so much taller. And now, these beautiful actresses in their medieval costumes and high headdresses looked so magnificent, without being intimidating. They were all very loving and protective of her. All Molly had to do on stage was to play with some fake deer while the 'grown-ups' worked their way through their drama, bring some wild berries in a basket to Genoveva, then stay in her arms and enjoy the motherly cuddling. Not very difficult for Molly to do as she often missed her own mother's cuddling.

Being part of a play, with colourful costumes and convincing forest and cave sceneries, opened up a whole new world for Molly. It was a strange world of make-believe. But, wasn't her stay at the boarding school not also a world of make-believe? A world of 28 girls in a dormitory and a dining room and a single school room, from grades one to eight, and an enclosed courtyard as playground, with only nuns as authority figures and caregivers. Oh, and one priest, of course, to cultivate their young souls with daily rituals in the chapel. No parents anywhere in sight. Lots of sisters, but no parents. Some of the girls were able to go home for the holidays and return at the start of school again; others, like herself, were there year-round. Some were half-orphans, like herself, and they were there because the remaining parent could not take care of them at home. Still others had rich and busy parents who simply didn't have time for their children but wanted them to get a solid education.

Molly briefly pondered the name Schmerzensreich, or Sorrowful. Although that boy lived in the woods for seven years with just a mother and friendly deer before being reunited with his father in the castle, it didn't seem to be an unhappy existence, at least not from the viewpoint of living in a boarding school.

But even living a very sheltered life in a Catholic boarding school, Molly would never consider herself 'Sorrowful.' Yes, life was impersonal and strict and regimented, but not painful or sorrowful. Every so often, the uniformed girls were marched along the country road outside the compound, seven rows of four, with the nuns alongside to keep them in line. They would walk along meadows and stare in wonderment at the grazing cows, being told that that's where milk came from. Being city girls, they had never seen cows before, and no matter how hard they looked, they could not find any source of milk on these animals. How, and where? Sometimes they would also be taken to a nearby forest to pick up beech nuts from the ground which would then be sent somewhere to extract oil from them. While in the forest, Molly loved picking pale green sour clover that grew in the shade under the trees and eating it, and she enjoyed her mouth puckering up, giving her an unusual sensation.

Although she had played Schmerzensreich, or Sorrowful, on stage, Molly decided that she did not identify with him. On the contrary: She was Mollina Tarin, a little girl with a future, hoping to grow taller, looking forward to a life yet to be lived, perhaps to be rescued by a prince to live happily ever after in a grand castle.

✝ ✝ ✝

One Of The Good Guys

Gordon had performed the song many times—in fact, every week for the past few months—about being 'one of the good guys,' resisting temptation at all costs, always staying on the straight and narrow. He had always sung it proudly, inwardly patting himself on the shoulder, seeing himself reflected in the main character.

But tonight was different. As he was singing before the audience in the hotel lounge, something about the whole concept bothered him... but what? He was still the same wholesome, faithful, ideal husband and family man that he had been for the past twenty-something years. He and his lovely wife still loved each other, even though they were edging into their middle years, and they were proud of their now grown children.

Then Gordon remembered how the whole thing had started. He was singing about this man walking alone on a beautiful beach, far away from home, at a convention. Suddenly he saw a woman standing at the edge of the water, letting the waves wash back and forth across her bare feet. He watched mesmerized as her long, golden hair was billowing in the soft breeze. She turned, and as they stood face to face, they both realized an instant connection between them. It was more than mere attraction; it was an inexplicable, deep connection. Silently, and in wonderment, they gazed into each other's eyes, holding hands, trembling slightly. Softly, she began to caress his face and leaned forward to kiss him.

He pulled away. NO! He would not be tempted to give in—he would never betray his wife, because he was 'one of the good guys!' Although the beach was totally deserted, and nobody would ever know of his indiscretion if he gave in, he would not allow himself to enjoy this perfect moment with a beautiful, willing stranger. After all, he was 'one of the good guys.'

As he was singing tonight, Gordon heard a sad "aahh!" from a lady in the front row. He glanced down without missing a beat, then promptly forgot about it.

Until the supper buffet tonight in the hotel restaurant. As he was filling his plate, a lady across the salad display called him. "Gordon!"

"What?" he asked impatiently, looking at her. "WHAT?"

"I will always remember you—as one of the good guys," she said.

"Yes, always!" he answered, still impatient for some reason. Then he emphasized, "forever and ever!"—not realizing how defensive he sounded.

"But—does it really matter?" she asked, ignoring his grumpiness.

"What?" Gordon asked again, with an angry look.

"I mean—the man will keep thinking about that long golden hair billowing in the breeze, whether he resisted temptation, or whether he allowed himself to indulge in the pleasure," the lady explained. "Either way, he will remember her and, secretly in his mind, he will make love to her. The mind has a way of playing tricks like that. So—does it really matter whether he is one of the good guys? If he commits adultery in his mind only, and nobody ever knows, will he still be one of the good guys?"

Gordon didn't answer but simply walked away. Why was he so angry? Because someone dared ask whether strict morals really mattered? Of course they mattered! Of course, being one of the good guys really mattered! With his Methodist lifestyle, there was never a question about stepping outside of the box.

He truly loved his wife, and he would never cheat on her... But deep in the recesses of his mind he knew that he had occasionally lusted after other women... hadn't all men? And why was he suddenly thinking about living in a box? Perhaps the sad "aahh..." and the lady's questions had forced such secret and repressed thoughts to the surface.

Was he so angry because he had to confront the idea that, deep down, he may not be 'one of the good guys?' Did he secretly think about billowing hair without admitting it even to himself? Deep down, did he resent living in a box, year in and year out, just because he prided himself being 'one of the good guys?' If that was the case, weren't his morals based on the wrong motivation?

Perhaps the lady had a point, he thought, chewing on his salad. Whether you give in to temptation or resist it, the outcome is the same—you keep thinking about it. Your mind is contaminated either way. So—where was the dividing line?

Why had he added "forever and ever" earlier? Did he try to convince himself that he was 'one of the good guys?' And if he wasn't, in the final, painful, soul-searching tally, and nobody else knew, did it really matter?

✝ ✝ ✝

"On he whole, human beings want to be good,
but not too good, and not quite all the time."

—George Orwell

Two Intimate Strangers

While the hotel guests were waiting in the comfortable lounge for the elegant dining room to open, one of the guests was delighting the international crowd nightly with his piano stylings. There were always a few dedicated music lovers around the beautiful grand piano, grateful for the unexpected entertainment.

One evening, when most people had already left for the dining room, one elegant blonde lady with a cane lingered at the piano, along with me, and she kept raving about the sensitivity and soul of that music. Finally I asked her, "Do you play an instrument yourself?"

"No, unfortunately not," she replied. "I started learning the piano as a child when I lived with my family in Sicily. But then my piano teacher died suddenly, and as he was the only qualified teacher in Sicily at the time, that was the end of my music studies. I wanted to continue them in Milan, but my father wouldn't let me. So that was that!" And she sighed a heavy sigh. "I could have been very good. I could play with soul, like him," she added, with a nod to the pianist.

"I guess the piano was not in the cards for you," I joked.

"What do you mean, 'in the cards'?" she inquired. "I don't understand."

"Well, they say that you're born with a hand of cards, and that you have to play those cards to the best of your abilities," I tried to explain. "So maybe there was no piano in your cards."

"You mean, like destiny, or fate?"

"I suppose you could call it that," I conceded.

"But was it my destiny to end up like this?" she asked, pointing to her cane. "Do you realize how it has changed my life, having to walk with a cane? I, a professional woman, a successful business-woman! I own two well-known fashion stores, one for ladies clothes, the other for sexy lingerie. I was at the top of my game! Successful in business and socially. And then this! Why me? WHY ME???" There was an ocean of pain and distress in her voice.

"Do you still live in Sicily?" I asked, in a futile attempt to distract her away from her pain and self-pity.

"Oh no, I've lived in Milan for many years now, and my busi-nesses are in Milan," she said. "That's what makes it worse, having to move in our social circles like this!"

Pointing to her cane, I dared ask, "So what happened?" She didn't have to answer if she didn't want to.

"My doctor misdiagnosed me for two years," she recalled bitterly, seeming eager to tell me. "When I first went to him with my hip pain, he didn't bother to check thoroughly and just prescribed some pills. But the pain kept getting worse, and I kept going back to him for further tests, but he never took it seriously. Finally, after two years of back and forth, some in-depth test revealed bone cancer, and they had to remove several inches of bone from that leg. That's why my one leg is so much shorter than the other, and I need the cane."

"When was that?" I inquired.

"It has been nine years now," she lamented. "Nine years of looking like this! Fortunately, my husband and two sons have been very supportive. But what's the point of continuing like this?"

Oh, my God! This beautiful, elegant, middle-aged lady had been carrying around that bitterness and self-pity for nine years! Wasn't it high time for her to snap out of this paralyzing and toxic mental state?

The pianist had long gone to dinner and we were the only two people left in the lobby. So I reached for her hand and asked, "What's your name?"

She seemed to ponder that question for a while, so I said, "My name is Mollina Tarin, but please call me Molly."

"I'm Tina," she finally whispered.

"Madame Tina," I said, still holding her hand, "has it ever occurred to you that all this might have had a purpose?"

She looked at me wide-eyed. "How could there be a purpose in my misery?" Her eyes started filling with tears. "Or—do you mean there is hope? — My God, I'm starting to cry!"

"That's OK—go ahead and cry," I reassured her. "Nobody else is here now. They've all gone to dinner."

She went to sit down on a sofa, and I joined her. For a while, we sat there in silence.

"Please tell me: what purpose could there possibly be?" she insisted.

"Well, it looks to me that you're too young to have played all your cards yet. There are still cards in your deck that haven't been played," I suggested.

"Oh, Miss Molly, please explain," she pleaded with tears in her eyes. "Please tell me! I must know what I should do!"

"I cannot tell you what to do. But it seems that your life at this point has reached an impasse. You have made it on a material level. I don't know what's in store for you, but it may be time for you to move to another level, perhaps move into an entirely different direction."

Again clutching my hand, she was clearly thinking about all this. So I continued with my thought. "You said that your family has been wonderful through all this, yet you keep focusing on a nine-year-old problem. As long as you don't get past what happened many years ago, you are not able to move ahead. Can you walk without a cane?"

"Yes, I can, but it's more comfortable with it."

"Yes, your cane has become a permanent crutch for you, and that in turn doesn't let you forget your bitterness and self-pity. No—don't get upset! I'm simply stating a fact. Right?" She seemed to calm down again. "Right! But you can move beyond that state and become greater than your problem…"

She seemed mesmerized, hungrily taking it all in, hanging on my every word. "Oh, how lucky I am to meet you—yes, I see that I HAD to meet you!

"Destiny again! I'm here only for three days and you for one week, and we meet! And I don't even like this hotel! Now that's destiny! So—please go on, Miss Molly! Please!"

"Remember Christopher Reeve, the American actor who played Superman?" I asked, and she nodded. "And remember his riding accident that left him paralyzed to a point where he needed machinery to help him breathe? When he had nothing to look forward to but a seemingly useless life in a wheelchair, totally at the mercy of a team of caregivers to look after his every need?" Again she nodded.

"Well, when he first realized the hopelessness of his situation, he wanted to end it all and save his family a lot of heartache. He changed his mind only when he saw the love in the eyes of his wife and children who wanted him to live. In other words, he stayed in the WHY ME? stage for only a very short time before he moved on." I paused to let that sink in, then continued.

"Luckily, he was rich enough to get the very best medical team to help him improve, even just marginally, but enough to set himself a goal. And in the short time he had left to live, he became the spokesperson for the thousands of people with the same severe spinal cord injuries, and he managed to raise enormous funds for research into that field, giving hope to those thousands who were then without hope.

"Imagine if he had decided to just feel sorry for himself and give up at the beginning, his family and the world would have missed out on a great role model. The research into spinal cord injuries would still be nowhere, and thousands of sufferers would still have no hope for recovery, ever…"

I paused again to see if she was still following my thoughts. When she squeezed my hand, with eyes shining, I continued.

"But here is the point of interest for you: When he was at his pinnacle, at the top of his career, with a beautiful family, it probably never occurred to him that his life would suddenly change direction, and so drastically. He had it all. Why would he change anything? But his accident changed EVERYTHING! He could either give up, or be useful. And it is possible that, in his final, painful years, he fulfilled his purpose in life. He could have chosen otherwise, but didn't. Perhaps he realized that he still had another role to play, another type of Superman."

"That's what I mean when I say that you still hold cards you haven't played yet. I don't know what they are, and you won't find out what they are or what kind of destiny is yours to live before you get yourself out of your nine-year victim mode groove. Nothing new can come to you until you get rid of the old. You are still a very beautiful woman, intelligent and successful, so you have a lot going for you if you choose to use it!"

Tina squeezed my hand again, with tears in her eyes. "You have no idea how I needed to hear such a positive message! You gave me so much to think about! How can I ever thank you? When I think… Nobody at home would ever dare talk to me like that—but I really needed to hear it. Oh, destiny again!" Excitedly, her words fairly tumbled out of her. "Oh—it will be so exciting to think about all that! Thank you, Miss Molly, thank you!"

She finally let go of my hand, carefully blotted the last tears off her carefully applied make-up, checked her face and hair in her bejeweled little hand mirror, then gave me a reserved hug. "I will give you my address in Milan, and next time you come to Milan, you won't have to stay in any hotel because you will stay at my house. Oh, I do hope you come to visit me in Milan!"

Finally, we both proceeded to the dining room, two intimate strangers, back in our hotel guest roles.

✝ ✝ ✝

Boys Will Be Boys

Once upon a time there were two boys, Alfie and Bertie—ordinary boys, with crooked teeth and freckles and dirty hands and pockets full of string and pinecones and, sometimes, frogs.

"I can run faster than you," Alfie challenged Bertie. "Not so," said Bertie, and started running, with Alfie right behind him. They both finished at the same time, and they laughed.

"I can jump higher than you," Bertie challenged Alfie. "Not so," said Alfie, and jumped the backyard fence, with Bertie jumping the same fence equally effortlessly, and they laughed.

Their competitiveness was constant and inexhaustible. They always managed to come up with new, more creative challenges, from spitting cherry stones farther, to landing more balls in the makeshift basket, to anything else they could think of. But, somehow, there was never a clear winner, which spurned them on to ever more outlandish feats. And they always laughed.

One day, messing around by the pond, Alfie cornered Bertie. "I bet you $10 that you can't do what I'm going to do," he challenged.

"Ten bucks! That's my whole weekly allowance! But—I bet you $10 that I can do the same thing, whatever it is," countered Bertie.

Alfie reached into his pocket and took out a reluctant frog, dangled it in front of his grimacing face, then swallowed the frog. "Give me the $10!"

Perplexed, Bertie slowly handed over the $10, and scratched his head. Finally, he reached into his pocket, took out a squirming frog and said angrily, "When I swallow this frog, you give me back my $10!" And with a disgusted gulp, he swallowed the frog.

Alfie handed Bertie back his $10, and they both looked at each other, horrified. It had suddenly dawned on them that they had each swallowed a frog, for NOTHING! And, almost simultaneously, they bent down and threw up.

But, for the first time, they didn't laugh.

‡

Once upon a time, not so long ago, there were three major newspapers in the mega-city. Then, one day, with great fanfare, a fourth newspaper came on the scene, threatening the cherished profits of the other three.

They didn't need more competition; it was already a cutthroat business. What to do? The big boys in their corner offices huddled in conferences, brainstorming. How could they outsmart their competitors? How could they preserve their slice of the pie—perhaps even increase it? One thing for sure: nobody wanted a smaller slice.

Then, one day, newspaper A came up with its trump card: it would print and distribute free tabloid-sized teasers to increase its readership. It was aiming at transit riders who didn't normally buy a newspaper, to get them interested in daily reading and, hopefully, in buying the full newspaper eventually.

However, newspaper B soon followed what seemed like a good idea. It printed and distributed its own free tabloid-sized teasers, aimed at the same non-buying transit riders.

Soon thereafter, newspaper C, not wanting to be left behind in the dust, copied the same idea. By now, newspaper boxes with all the freebies were to be found everywhere, vying for the same readership.

It soon became apparent that most of the transit riders who so voraciously picked up, read and discarded these freebies, never did end up buying the full newspapers, despite aggressive telephone marketing campaigns to supplement the freebies. So, reluctantly, the big boys in their corner offices decided to cut their losses before the damage became irreparable.

Today, only newspaper A still offers the freebies, while newspapers B and C retreated from the competitive battle long ago, no doubt licking their wounds and mopping up the red ink.

Will boys never learn? When will they stop swallowing frogs?

✝ ✝ ✝

"When everyone thinks alike,
no one thinks very much."

—Anon

The Mystery of the Leg

"Would you believe what this actress did when they amputated her leg?" my desk mate Gerry asked me one day. Gerry was a celebrity writer at the tabloid newspaper where we both worked, and he knew almost everything there was to know about anybody worthy of a good headline.

"No—but I'm sure you're eager to tell me," I replied. He leaned across his typewriter and laughed.

"These people are nuts, I tell you," he said, almost conspiratorially. "You'd think that losing a leg would be horrible enough, especially if you're making a living as a stage actress. But this one was so full of herself that she had a white baby casket made to put her leg in so that she could properly mourn it."

I thought about that for a minute. "Well, I guess the leg had served her well on stage, and she found it proper to give it the send-off it deserved," I ventured. "Who was she, anyway?"

"Her name was Sarah Bernhardt, and she died in Paris in 1923, at age 79," Gerry said. "She was considered one of the greatest actresses of her time, generally making good money. And when times were lean, she apparently switched from a standing position on stage to a horizontal one in bed to keep herself in luxury, if you know what I mean," he added with a wink.

Gerry was again rummaging through the office filing cabinets for more juicy tidbits. Back in the 1970, before computers and Internet, background files on just about any topic could be found in the newspaper's filing cabinets. The newspaper employed 'clippers' that scoured newspapers from around the world every day for articles that might be of use to us writers for whatever stories we were assigned to handle. Writing about Sarah Bernhardt's leg in a baby casket had sent him to her folder in the filing cabinet for further details.

"Oh—listen to this," Gerry exclaimed with glee. "It says here that, to help her understand and feel the tragedies that she needed to act out on stage, she often slept in a coffin instead of in a bed, and that she and her coffin became famous."

"I presume that when she wanted company, she would have to sleep in a bed," I suggested. "I don't think that they had coffins for two with room enough to romp around."

"Well, she would have been eccentric enough to have a double coffin made for such pleasures," Gerry added, and we both laughed and went back to work at our typewriters.

✝

Many years later, when my dear friend Babs was forced to consider leg amputation, I wanted to find role models for her to demonstrate that her life would not end, but that there had been people over the years that lived productive lives after amputation. I was thinking of Terry Fox who ran thousands of miles across Canada with a prosthetic leg to raise money for cancer. I remembered Ella Fitzgerald, one of the greatest jazz singers ever, who needed to have a leg amputated, and who later even lost her eyesight to diabetes, but who continued singing on stage.

Then I remembered Gerry's story, and I started to research Sarah Bernhardt on the Internet.

It seems that this dramatic actress of 100 years ago was neither particularly beautiful nor superbly talented, but that she had a voice of gold, and that she had that magical ability to keep her audiences mesmerized. That's why she was called The Divine Sarah. She played many famous roles on stage, including many male roles such as a celebrated Hamlet. At age 56 she played Napoleon's 21-year-old son who dies in *L'Aiglon* which was a patriotic tragedy written for her. It probably helped that she was openly bisexual.

It was in the stage play of *La Tosca*—a play that Puccini later turned into an opera—where she injured her knee. In the final scene, Tosca is required to jump off a high wall, usually onto a hidden mattress, and the nightly jumps damaged her right knee to such an extent that she ended up in constant pain because the knee failed to heal properly. Finally, gangrene started to set in, and so at age 71 she ordered her right leg amputated.

It is reported that, while sinking into the anesthetic, she sang the French patriotic song, La Marseillaise. Considering her eccentricity, this actually sounds true!

Now the mystery about her leg really starts.

Apparently, the Divine Sarah got an offer of $10,000—a huge amount of money 100 years ago!—to publicly display her amputated leg, but she refused the offer.

Then there is the story about the white baby casket made to rest her amputated leg for proper mourning. Perhaps that's when she got the offer of $10,000 to display it more publicly.

But just recently, a leg was discovered in a storeroom in a Bordeaux University in France, and the controversy still rages whether or not this is the Divine Sarah's amputated leg, still preserved in formaldehyde. There are two questions: Why and how was the leg lost for 94 years? And why is the knee missing, if the leg was amputated because of a diseased knee? Perhaps for research? The university denies the suggestion that the leg was ever missing.

In the meantime, just a few months after the amputation, the Divine Sarah was back on stage playing *La Dame aux Camelias* in a wheelchair. Back in those days, prosthetic limbs were made of wood and much less sophisticated than they are today. So whenever the wooden leg bothered her, she switched to the wheelchair and moved around the stage in that chair. This play was later turned into the opera *La Traviata* by Verdi.

Sarah Bernhardt continued working on stage for another few years, using either her wooden leg or her wheelchair, until her death in Paris in 1923, at age 79.

✝ ✝ ✝

The Final Affection

At a time when Living Wills and other pre-death decisions are still hot and controversial topics, I continue to be strongly influenced by the death of my mother in the late 1980s.

When people call me headstrong and independent, I must tell them that I'm only a tiny chip off the old block. If I think of my mother as being the ultimate independent one, I have to remind myself that she was only a watered-down version of her own mother who had lived alone for decades in her tiny apartment until she was finally committed to an old folks home at age 93, where she died of sheer frustration a mere 10 days later.

Decades ago, my mother had turned into a seemingly happy hermit, living alone with her books and her television and dozens of plants, about 3,000 miles away from my home in Canada. When she started getting forgetful, her good friends and neighbors living in the apartment above made sure that she got three warm meals every day, and a social worker took care of her finances and kept an eye on the total situation.

One day my mother fell in her apartment. Although she was not seriously hurt, the social worker took her to the hospital and decided that it was time for mother to move into the spacious, modern nursing home next to the hospital, where she could be cared for 24 hours a day, if necessary.

The move triggered the memory of my rebellious grandmother who simply would not adjust to dependent living. Daily I called my sister who lived a four-hour drive away from mother: Was mother adjusting? Would it be necessary for me to book an imme-diate flight at a moment's notice?

Fortunately, mother adjusted less rebelliously. Oh, she wandered away a few times, but each time she was returned by some good Samaritans who read the name and address label on her clothes— the label being attached at the back where mother could not reach to remove it. Sometimes she took a taxi back to her old address, an apartment where other people now lived; but as she had no money, the driver returned her to the home to get paid.

It also took mother a while to get used to having other people watching television with her in the common room; at first, she chased everybody out of what she thought was her living room and locked the door. "What nerve of them to just walk into MY living room!" she would protest to the attendant who had to persuade her to share the television.

When she finally settled in, more or less, I booked a flight to visit her. At first, she was not sure who I was and assumed I was my sister. Then it dawned on her that I had come all the way from Canada to visit her—not exactly an annual occurrence. She felt mixed emotions: on the one hand, very happy to see me; on the other hand, guilty about having imposed a financial burden on me.

I spent two weeks with her, visiting her daily, although she would usually dismiss me—or us, when my sister came along— after a relatively short time. She had slimmed down considerably since I last saw her, and her hair was now pure white, framing her wrinkled face in a soft and strangely flattering bob haircut.

Osteoporosis had stooped mother quite severely, and she was not able to walk more than a few feet at a time without resting. Coupled with incontinence, this presented a problem when any distance away from her room or a washroom. On one visit, we were escorting her to a washroom when she stopped and exclaimed, "Oh, oh—it's too late!" So we returned her to her room to get her changed into dry underwear. While my sister walked over to the window to admire the spectacular mountain view, I proceeded to look after mother's needs. She dutifully lifted her dress to let me wash and dry her and change her diaper.

While this complete role reversal seemed the most natural thing for me to do and for her to accept, I was shocked at the change in her attitude: I had never seen any naked part of my mother's body because she had always been the world's most prudish prude. Now, without any hesitation or shame, she exposed herself to me, her daughter, in such a totally natural and innocent manner that I was taken aback. My mother, always so proud and unbending and domineering and prude, now had become the little girl she had probably never been, never was allowed to be around her own proud and domineering mother—just so innocent and natural.

This little incident created turmoil in my mind. I felt sorry for her, for having been compelled to lead a lonely life, however self-imposed, because she had never allowed herself to show any affection or to accept the physical aspects of human life. I felt compassion for her, for not having known how to break the chains of her own mother's domination and influence, for not realizing and coming to terms with all that. Although, like me, she had moved far away from her mother to lead her own life, somehow she had never really broken loose. Somehow she had remained in the mold of her puritanical upbringing.

The days went by. Each day she finally recognized me, without remembering that I had been there the day before, and the day before that. At every visit she saw me for the first time, and there was always, finally, the joy of recognition. Then she would plead with me to take her back to her old apartment, where other people now lived. To persuade her to stay, I always had to lie to her, tell her that others were on their way over to see her. And she always cried when I left.

My sister could not cope with the situation. Already prone to depression, she always ended up very depressed, and she was glad that I, the strong one, was with her. She could not cope with mother's incontinence because it reminded her of her own older husband for whom she had cared until he died. Sometimes even I would cry on the way home.

Towards the end of my stay, mother had finally realized that I was really visiting her from Canada, and that her condition had to be pretty bad. There were times when she was aware of how far her mind had slipped—when she was aware of the hopelessness of her situation. But those were also the moments when, for the first time since my very early childhood, she showed me any affection. For the first time that I could remember, we were holding hands, and she allowed me to stroke her soft, white hair.

Exactly one week after my return to Canada, my mother died. According to a friend who continued to visit her, she never opened her eyes again after I left. Deep in my heart I have always known that she just gave up after my departure, having realized WHY I had visited her. I am sure she knew that she would never see me again, and that she simply had nothing left to look forward to, nothing left to live for. So she just gave up, never opened her eyes again, and died.

After her death, I was again in turmoil: On the one hand I was happy that she would not have to vegetate for months or years to come; on the other hand I was angry—oh, so angry!—at the indignities nature imposes on so many older people. I was angry because we are kinder to animals; we don't let them suffer the same way. We humans, because we consider ourselves superior to animals, must suffer until they disconnect the machinery or discontinue the treatments, unless someone is strong-willed enough to simply stop living the way my mother did. I was angry that old age can destroy the mind and the dignity of a person, even a strong and proud person such as my mother had been.

Life has gone on, but my perspective on life changed drastically when my mother died. I know I don't want to suffer the same indignities. I want to make the most of life while I still can. I want to take steps to die in dignity. I want to make the most of precious relationships. I want to show my loved ones that I love them; I want to show my affection.

Thinking of my mother simply giving up after I left her, I realize now that this was her rare and final act of affection for me.

(1991)

✝ ✝ ✝

We, The Slaves

Do you realize that we are all slaves?

Oh, I'm not talking about the traditional meaning of slavery where rich and powerful people owned poor and defenseless people, although in some countries that kind of slavery still exists to this very day.

No—I'm talking about the fact that, especially in our incredibly advanced society, we are all slaves of something, or someone.

Just think about it. If we become dependent on, or addicted to, something or someone, we are not self-reliant any more, and we have become slaves of that something or someone. In other words: WHO or WHAT is in control? If it controls you, you're a slave of it. It can be food, television, sports, sex, smoking, money, ambition, the Internet, gambling... There are so many types of enslavement, that probably all of us are victims of some of them. I will mention just a few.

For example: Can you start functioning in the morning without your coffee, or tea, or a cigarette, or a sugar fix? Can you get through your day without any number of coffees, or teas, or nicotine, or drinks? You may be a slave not only of caffeine, or nicotine, or alcohol, but also of the ritual of drinking, or of smoking.

Many years ago, after some kind soul had taught me how to play Solitaire, I became addicted to that card game. I would rush home from work, sit down on the floor with my cards without even taking off my shoes or coat, and start playing Solitaire. When I finally became aware of that addiction I immediately quit, and I have never touched another card since. Whenever I refuse to play cards with friends, they don't understand, but I don't owe them any explanation.

And how many of us are addicted to our watches? How often do you look at your watch throughout the day, even when time doesn't matter? Do you look at your watch to decide whether it's time to eat? Has looking at your watch become an enslaving ritual, or habit, for you? When I first started this game many years ago, I realized that I was a slave to my watch, so I didn't wear a watch for six months just to prove that I could get along without one, if necessary.

Now, technology is a wonderful thing—but to what extent have we come to rely on it? If we depend on gadgets to do the work for us, have we not become slaves to those gadgets? If we have, we are not self-reliant anymore. Just think of the proliferation of cell phones and their constantly upgraded versions…

Another example: How many of us are slaves to our cars? Cars have become extensions of ourselves, in many cases replacing our feet for even short distances, even when public transportation is available.

Or take ambition, or money, or possessions. Being a slave to ambition or money or possessions means that you're never happy with what you've got—you always want more. And you can never win because there will always be others who have more. No, there is nothing wrong with balanced ambition, but it will be a never-ending quest until you become aware of the futility of always just wanting more for the sake of wanting.

Habits themselves can be very enslaving. Of course, we need habits—or rituals—to simplify and structure our lives. Without them, we would have chaos. But people who let habits rule their lives often become inflexible and boring, because they don't allow any room for change and personal growth.

In our lifetime, many of us become so emotionally involved with another person that it can lead to emotional enslavement. Allow me to quote the Indian mystic and philosopher Bhagwan Shree Rajneesh (1931–1990), from *The Book of the Books*, Vol. IV:

"If you depend on someone for your happiness...
...you depend on so many people:
They all become subtle masters
They all exploit you in return."

Of course, when we commit to a close relationship with another person, there is obviously an emotional involvement. But when carried too far, leaving no space to the other, it becomes obsession, and therefore bondage, or enslavement. This type of emotional addiction can be very painful when people don't want to let go and, one way or another, this creates distress. As we regularly hear on the news, the result is often some horrific violence.

Then, some time ago I realized that I had become a news junkie. As our world keeps shrinking with all the new technology and exposing us to literally every corner of our globe, it is very tempting to want to know everything that's going on. This can become an unnecessary habit, and I had to break away from constantly flipping channels to make sure I got news from all around the world. I had to realize that the world continues to function without my watching every development, and that my watching made absolutely no difference on how the world turns.

Right now, I still LOVE food! Although I'm a healthy and discerning eater, I LOVE FOOD, and as my cooking is very tasty, it's hard to cut back. Probably emotional eating, no doubt a remnant of some still unresolved emotional trauma from a while back. As a result, there is more of me than there was a few years ago... Oh, did I mention that I LOVE FOOD? This one is a real challenge.

Now, I take personal inventory periodically to try and nip any new enslaving habits in the bud, but I don't always succeed. And here's another problem: As soon as I get rid of one enslavement— oops!—there pops up another. I guess, vigilance is the word.

Have you ever taken stock? If you haven't, I'd like to challenge you to try it, in the privacy of your own mind, of course, and you might be surprised at what you find -- if you are totally honest with yourself, that is.

After all, nobody wants consciously to be a slave. But human nature being what it is, it will be a life-long battle.

✝ ✝ ✝

The Power Of One

It was early Saturday evening and she was still riding high emotionally after a full day listening to an enthralling speaker at a four-day conference. She had no plans for the evening, and she didn't want to spoil the mood of the day by dining alone, or sitting in a bar sipping some drink she didn't want.

On the spur of the moment, she decided to check the evening's program at the prestigious concert hall located just a few blocks away from the conference hall and her hotel. Ah, some young Russian pianist playing Brahms, the *Piano Concerto No. 1*— wonderful! Although she was not familiar with this particular piano concerto, this would surely provide an appropriately peaceful and reflective ending to an exhilarating day. She quickly phoned the box office and reserved one of the very few seats left, then grabbed a sandwich and walked over to the concert hall.

Her seat was in the third row front and centre, normally a bit too close for a symphony concert, but with an excellent view of the pianist. She studied the program. Evgeny Kissin, a 37-year-old Russian, one of the legends of the piano world, with already a vast output of CDs and many international concert tours and numerous prestigious awards, including an Honorary Doctorate of Music, under his belt. What an unexpected evening this was promising to be!

Her seat mate on the left turned out to be a doctor from the East Coast, also in town for a conference, and they chatted for a while before the start of the concert. But once the music began, everyone sat enraptured by the intensity of the pianist and the flawless brilliance of his playing. Studying his face, she found great sadness, even a certain melancholy in his features; perhaps this was why he was able to lose himself so completely in his music. She speculated that traveling around the world on a concert tour would undoubtedly be very lonely and thus contribute to his melancholy.

At the end of his performance, there was the usual applause. 'That's not enough—this pianist was brilliant' she decided and stood up, continuing to clap. She was the only one standing; even her doctor seat mate refused to stand. The woman in the seat behind her poked her in the back and hissed, "Sit down—I can't see!" She turned around and suggested, "No—YOU stand up!" She continued standing and clapping, and the pianist gave her a surprised glance. She looked around and saw that other people were now standing up and applauding, and within less than one minute everybody in the hall, all 2,000 people at the orchestra level and the balconies, were standing and applauding, except the woman in the seat behind her who remained seated, probably out of spite.

The pianist continued to bow and thank the audience, looking totally fatigued and ready to collapse after his passionate and exhausting performance. Every time he bowed, she feared that he might topple over, but he supported himself at the piano, although he could barely keep his eyes open. Finally he left the stage, but the audience kept applauding until he returned and played an encore.

After the encore she stood up again, and all 2,000 people followed her in yet another standing ovation. He briefly left the stage, but once again the audience called him back for another encore.

After three encores and more standing ovations, she started feeling slightly guilty for draining even more of his waning energies. But she also knew that he would always remember this particular performance because he seemed surprised at the 12-minute standing ovation from a seemingly unexpected enthusiastic audience. Many performers are warned about the sometimes very reserved receptions in Canada, but this one was certainly an exception.

She was happy and a bit overwhelmed at the realization that one person alone—herself—was able to raise the energy level single-handedly in such a large concert hall, and turn an average reception into an electrified and memorable one for performer and audience alike.

Just another proof of the Power of One.

✝ ✝ ✝